SHORTCUT 7
306 HAPPINESS QUOTES

by LINKED IN AND TOWN HALL ACHIEVER OF THE YEAR
EY NOMINEE ENTREPRENEUR OF THE YEAR
GRAND HOMAGE LYS DIVERSITY
WORLD TOP100 DOCTORS

Dr BAK NGUYEN, DMD

TO ALL THOSE ACTIVELY SEEKING THEIR HAPPINESS, THEIR WAY HOME

by Dr BAK NGUYEN

ISBN: 978-1-989536-81-0

Published by: Dr. BAK PUBLISHING COMPANY
Dr.BAK 0099

DISCLAIMER

« The general information, opinions and advice contained in this medium and/or the books, audiobooks, podcasts and publications on Dr. Bak Nguyen's (legal name Dr. Ba Khoa Nguyen) website or social media (hereinafter the "Opinions") present general information on various topics. The Opinions are intended for informational purposes only.

No information contained in the Opinions is a substitute for an expert, consultation, advice, diagnosis or professional treatment. No information contained in the Opinions is a substitute for professional advice and should not be construed as consultation or advice.

Nothing in the Opinions should be construed as professional advice related to the practice of dentistry, medical advice or any other form of advice, including legal or financial advice, professional opinion, care or diagnosis, but strictly as general information. All information from the Opinions is for informational purposes only.

Any user who disagrees with the terms of this Disclaimer should immediately cease using or referring to the Opinions. Any action by the user in connection with the information contained in the Opinions is solely at the user's discretion.

The general information contained in the Opinions is provided "as is" and without warranty of any kind, either expressed or implied. Dr. Bak Nguyen (legal name Dr. Ba Khoa Nguyen) makes every effort to ensure that the information is complete and accurate. However, there is no guarantee that the general information contained in the Opinions is always available, truthful, complete, up-to-date or relevant.

The Opinions expressed by Dr. Bak Nguyen (legal name Dr. Ba Khoa Nguyen) are personal and expressed in his own name and do not reflect the opinions of his companies, partners and other affiliates.

Dr. Bak Nguyen (legal name Dr. Ba Khoa Nguyen) also disclaims any responsibility for the content of any hyperlinks included in the Opinions.

Always seek the advice of your expert advisors, physicians or other qualified professionals with any questions you may have regarding your condition. Never disregard professional advice or delay in seeking it because of something you have read, seen or heard in the Opinions. »

ABOUT THE AUTHOR

From Canada, **Dr. BAK NGUYEN**, Nominee Ernst and Young Entrepreneur of the year, Grand Homage Lys DIVERSITY, LinkedIn & TownHall Achiever of the year and TOP 100 Doctors 2021. Dr Bak is a cosmetic dentist, CEO and founder of Mdex & Co. His company is revolutionizing the dental field. Speaker and motivator, he wrote 72 books over 36 months accumulating many world records (to be officialized). His books are covering:

- **ENTREPRENEURSHIP**
- **LEADERSHIP**
- **QUEST OF IDENTITY**
- **DENTISTRY AND MEDICINE**
- **PARENTING**
- **CHILDREN'S BOOKS**
- **PHILOSOPHY**

In 2003, he founded Mdex, a dental company upon which in 2018, he launched the most ambitious private endeavour to reform the dental industry, Canada wide. Philosopher, he has close to his heart the quest of happiness of the people surrounding him, patients and colleagues alike. In 2020, he launched an International collaborative initiative named **THE ALPHAS** to share knowledge and for Entrepreneurs and Doctors to thrive through the Greatest Pandemic and Economic depression of our time.

In 2016, he co-found with Tranie Vo, Emotive World Incorporated, a tech research company to use technology to empower happiness and sharing. U.A.X. the ultimate audio experience is the landmark project on which the team is advancing, utilizing the technics of the movie industry and the advancement in ARTIFICIAL INTELLIGENCE to save the book industry and to upgrade the continuing education space.

These projects have allowed Dr Nguyen to attract interests from the international and diplomatic community and he is now the centre of a global discussion in the wellbeing and the future of the health profession. It is in that matter that he shares his thoughts and encourages the health community to share their own stories.

"It's not worth it go through it alone! Together, we stand, alone, we fall."

Motivational speaker and serial entrepreneur, philosopher and author, from his own words, Dr Nguyen describes himself as a dentist by circumstances, an entrepreneur by nature and a communicator by passion.

He also holds recognitions from the Canadian Parliament and the Canadian Senate.

SHORTCUT 7

306 HAPPINESS QUOTES

by Dr BAK NGUYEN

INTRODUCTION
BY Dr BAK NGUYEN

INTRODUCTION
by Dr. BAK NGUYEN

I would love to say that much have passed since my last introduction but that will be a lie. Actually, 6 days have passed since. 6 days, that's less than a week. I had the time to go on an interview with my good friend, Jonas Diop, to celebrate the landmark of writing **96 books within 48 months**.

Since my debut as a writer, I am collecting world records. I started with writing my first book within 2 weeks, to finish that month with the same book written in 2 different languages, French and English within a month. That was my debut in literature.

The literate people and the book industry did not like that. I am a driver and a business person. I am a racer and a competitor. I care about numbers and stats, the fewer words, the better. I was a misfit from day one.

But writing came to me as a blessing, allowing me to find closure and to heal. Then, I grew as I shared, more and more of my journeys and secrets. And then, I found **leadership** as I empowered you!

The journey that you are travelling, I know all too well, I've been there and done all of it myself. So for the first time in my life, I feel free and strangely, happy! Strangely because I am a **world-class lazy** guy. Writing books is not something that I will find naturally appealing. But it worked, and I was too lazy to find something else.

So I kept writing. I finished my first year, shy of the perfect mark (12 books in 12 months). I crossed the finished line with **9 books written in 12 months**. That was still a world record, but I liked the rounded numbers. I gave it all I had. I fuelled my momentum with all the emotions I have available, anger, frustration, regrets, even doubts, not to mention ambition.

On that matter, I have to confess that ambition did not help much, inspiration-wise. It is not because you want something that you will find the magic to do it in a way that is worth the words and narrative.

Anger, frustration, regrets, and doubts, I ground them to keep moving forward. So you know, grinding those is not to clean your slate, on the contrary, these contained emotions, as you are grinding them will splash and stain everything that you are, look, and touch. You are empowering your pain and sorrow.

But I wanted my world records with rounded numbers, so I pushed until I got to 15 books written within 15 months. I was proud of myself but barely survive the process. It was hard and not as fun as it may sound.

Then, something magic happened, William joined and gave me something else to fuel my momentum with: his love, and hope. He wanted to write with me. Together, we were happy, and we leveraged that magic. He empowered me as I empowered him.

Happiness brought us to new heights as we broke the *sound barrier* together, as co-author, as father and son. That got me to announce the world record of **36 books written within 18 months + 1 week**! I hate that + 1 week, but that is really what it was, I had to wait for William's Spring break to finish the 36th book.

Feeling happy brought me there. And, I must add, it brought me there with **style** and **ease**. After that, I kept surfing my momentum, but now lightened and freed from the drama, regrets, and doubts, I sailed with my **Confidence** and with an open mind and heart to embrace the present, one day at a time, day after day.

I went on to score with fluidity the landmark world record of **24 books written in 48 months**. That was confirming my average of writing 2 books a month since my awakening. It was easy and that was time I took for myself.

I kept going since it was fun and pleasant. And I was too lazy to stand in front of my own momentum anyway.

> "Don't stand in front of a river unless
> you are ready to clean up the flood."
> Dr. Bak Nguyen

It was ambition that pushed me forward, it was the fun of surfing my own momentum. All my ambition did was to set up the round numbers **checkpoints**. And then, COVID happened. That threw me off course. I kept writing but not at the same pace.

By June that year, I realized that I was behind, by much. I pressured myself, announcing on-air, on an international interview that if I wanted to keep my landmark world record writing book, I will need to write a book every 8 days for 8 weeks straight!

That was a joke. Worst, I will become a joke if I miss that one. So I wrote with some external motivation, other than fun and momentum.

I finished with an even better score than I predicted. I set that that landmark world record of **72 books written within 36 months**, writing the last 8 within 8 days on average for 8 straight weeks and I finished with 10 days prior to the dateline, August 31st!

Well, that's not all. I lied. I did not write a book every 8 days for 8 weeks straight, I wrote, edited, and published each of my written books during the same time! I don't even know how to express that in world record terms.

If the local book industry did not like me at my debut, well, my Momentum and boldness got me the recognition of **Apple Books**, **Amazon**, and, after that landmark record, the attention of **Barnes & Noble** too. These three, the big three became my biggest fans, supporters, and partners, publishing my books within days, even hours after my submission, book after book.

Well, last week, at 2 weeks from August 31st, 2021, all three were publishing my 96th book, making official my landmark and annual world record. But this year, ambition took over.

Last year, an Alpha and brother from another mother (that's how he called himself), Dr. Paul Ouellette suggested that I will be writing 100 books. That stayed in the back of my mind.

100 books, that is surely a great landmark, but how about the rounded numbers? 100 books in 50 months? Why not have some fun and make it 4 instead? Not 4 months, but 4 years. And that is the kind of player that I am.

That is the Pride on which I am paving my days lately, trying to get to that 100's mark. I had a little more than 2 weeks to deliver the 4 extra books and I must say that I was sprinting to get to the 96's mark.

The last sprint, I wrote and publish 4 of the **SHORTCUT volumes** within 10 days. I must say that I feel as exhausted as when I was trying to score **15 books in 15 months**.

I tried the old tricks and asked for William's help. He stood in to interview me for the writing of **TIMING, TIME MANAGEMENT ON STEROIDS**, my 74th book. 74th to replace **COVIDCONOMICS** that will not be ready in time. Thanks to William, I passed the checked point of 96/48.

Yesterday, with the publishing of the 6th volume of **SHORTCUT, POWER**, I still have 2 **SHORTCUT volumes** to write, **HAPPINESS** and **DOCTOR**, and 1 last book to replace

CRYPTOCONOMY that will also not be ready on time. So that is 3 books and I have 10 days left.

The odds are 3.33 days per book. In the last introduction, I was talking about 4.5 days per book. I just lost 36 hours per book! That will tell you much, not only about the pressure but also the accumulated fatigue, running a crazy race alone.

I am alone running but I am not isolated. More than the big three, **Apple Books**, **Amazon**, and **Barnes & Noble**, I now have a crowd of supporters on social media following my posts and story. Unlike the previous year, I do not feel the: ***"Wait for him to fail"*** vibe anymore. This year, people are cheering for me!

Most of them, I don't know. But all of them, I thank from the bottom of my heart. And this is where I am, standing at the end of my introduction for my 98th book.

This journey is about happiness and cheating, of course. Actually, I will cut to the chase. **I use happiness to cheat**! How about that for a shortcut? While common wisdom and culture like to define happiness as a destination, I am not as patient to sacrifice my life for the promise of happiness.

Instead, I will take whatever happiness I can found today and will surf with it. Intrigued? This is the journey ahead, a promising one, a fun one. That, I promise.

This is **Shortcut volume 7, Happiness**. Welcome to the Alphas.

Smile, that's the C major chord of the ballade.

Dr. BAK NGUYEN

PART 1

"HAPPINESS"

by Dr. BAK NGUYEN

Yesterday,
I was half the man I am Today
No more pain, no more sorrow
I left it all behind as I followed

I am twice because now, I am whole
That I know, because I am on a roll
I am ready for better, for more
Because now, I know my core

No more doubt, no more regret
I stand tall since I walked over my head
This journey got me away from the rain
Healing from the drama and drain
I am ready for better, for more
Because now, I know my core

I found my powers with you
And I left you a trail of cue
You just need to be ready
To find what you seek and be happy

You don't have to walk all the way
Before feeling happy,
You just need to dance and play
Since Confidence is sexy

I am ready for better, for more
Because now, I know my core

Happiness is not a destination
It is the theme of your perception
Now that I am whole
I am ready to be one, to merge my soul
With the Universe

I will be one
I will be powerful

Because now, I am happy and free

This is Shortcut volume 7 - Happiness

Can you think of a better way to start this final chapter with you? This is the 7th volume of the journey, of **SHORTCUT**. This one is about happiness.

After the last volume, the dark one about **POWER**, you have graduated and have already started your rise, healing, or growth. Don't rush, we each have our own timing and pace, this, this time, is not a race.

Only once out of your Quest of Identity (healing) can you start your rise. The preparation phase was growth and the journey starts with rising. From **Leadership**, **Confidence**, **Success** to **Power**, you have climbed the ladders and found your powers.

So this is the celebration of your ascension, the beginning of your legend. To you it is a journey, one to walk day after day. If you found your powers as I taught you, in the service of others, **resistance** will be shy and **jealousy** will be muted. Because you served, your story will be retold as a legend.

Not because it was propaganda but because to you, it was a walk, one step after the next. Because you served, you will get better at the task and do more and more. Because you did more and more, you also did better.

"Growing occurs at the giving end."
Dr. Bak Nguyen

That growth will elevate you into a legend. To them, it was not about what you are but what you did. That is what they have out of the trade, what you did and gave. But to you, your legend is all about who you are, what you have become.

From the legend, they kept the fruits, you kept the growth and the Confidence. Pretty great trade, if you ask me! And that is what we learnt so far, from waking up to heal, to grow, and to go out to rise, empowering and helping others.

Well, what's next? How do we keep that pace and keep evolving for more, for better? And this is the final chapter of the **SHORTCUT** franchise, **Happiness**. To keep moving forward, surf the fun and leverage happiness.

"We are what we feel. Our body produces the hormones that make or break our days and dream."
Dr. Bak Nguyen

This is quote 2521. Be happy, feel happy and you have all the power you need within you to move forward and to discover more fun, powers, and shapes. Don't be mistaken and fooled by the lies of dogma telling you that one day the reward will come.

We were all born happy. That was our natural state. We all know what happiness is. Some will be luckier and will be bathed in happiness. Some others will be tested heavily before they could find their way back to happiness. This is the narrative that we are fed, all of our lives, sacrifice now to be happy later. Well, here is a spoiler:

"Happiness is not a destination, it is a state of mind."
Dr. Bak Nguyen

This is quote 2522. You were born happy. You know what happiness is. Never forget that feeling, it will become the sun in each of your days.

I had my share of bad lucks and misery too. Those were facts. How I approached them was my choice. I was upset, I was frustrated, I was even angry. I used those emotions to fuel my momentum. It worked, but at what cost? I was grinding my soul at each turn. And do I have to tell you how fast I move? The pain was real and the turns stacking up faster than I can count.

It was powerful but did nothing for my **Healing**. Then, I tried something else, I try to purge the past, good and bad, and to look at the horizon. That day, I had a real choice, a real chance. I started with a clean slate. I loved the freedom and the lightness of that feeling.

I decided to leave the drama, the anger, the guilt behind to embrace **Gratitude** (which is the only past that I am keeping) and the **opportunity**. That day I felt happy, I felt free. That day, I became one with the **Forces of Nature** contained within me.

I became one and found *synergy* because I was finally available. And that is the secret of happiness. Not what happiness is but how to leverage happiness to ease your way.

You know me, I am not strong on definitions and too lazy anyway to address what is not absolutely necessary. And here is the journey ahead, of my **SHORTCUTS**, not to happiness, but for, and from, happiness.

This is **Shortcut volume 7, Happiness**. Welcome to the Alphas.

Dr. BAK NGUYEN

PART 2
"57 HAPPINESS QUOTES"
by Dr. BAK NGUYEN

1500
FROM SYMPHONY OF SKILLS
"Ease your mind and free your heart,
this is the way to happiness"
Dr. Bak Nguyen

1501
FROM IDENTITY, ANTHOLOGY OF QUESTS
"The pursuit of happiness is
the quest of the lost paradise, literally."
Dr. Bak Nguyen

1502
FROM IDENTITY, ANTHOLOGY OF QUESTS
"Happiness is the feeling to vibe freely,
tuned in with the universe."
Dr. Bak Nguyen

1503
FROM IDENTITY, ANTHOLOGY OF QUESTS
"Give yourself to the music, free your emotions
and you will experience lightness of one's soul!
Even sadness will feel beautiful!"
Dr. Bak Nguyen

1504

FROM IDENTITY, ANTHOLOGY OF QUESTS

"Strength is not happiness
and happiness is not weakness."

Dr. Bak Nguyen

1505

FROM IDENTITY, ANTHOLOGY OF QUESTS

"Smile, that's the C major chord of the ballade."

Dr. Bak Nguyen

1506

FROM IDENTITY, ANTHOLOGY OF QUESTS

"We were all profoundly and truly happy
at the beginning. We trust in ourselves,
we know the way home!"

Dr. Bak Nguyen

1507

FROM PROFESSION HEALTH

"Happiness is the result of an outcome that is either
equal to or better than the one expected."

Dr. Bak Nguyen

1508

FROM PROFESSION HEALTH

"In our quest for happiness, freedom is overrated."
Dr. Bak Nguyen

1509

FROM PROFESSION HEALTH

"Emotions, true and strong emotions are part of the deal of being human. So is happiness!"
Dr. Bak Nguyen

1510

FROM PROFESSION HEALTH

"An open mind will always achieve happiness faster than its alternative. Honestly, try it to be convinced!"
Dr. Bak Nguyen

1511

FROM PROFESSION HEALTH

"We need each other to be happy, so we, so you, so I, can be happy."
Dr. Bak Nguyen

1512

"To be happy, we must be human.
And humans are powerful!"

Dr. Bak Nguyen

1513

"Happiness is a dance.
It will remain as the music continues."

Dr. Bak Nguyen

1514

"No one can be truly happy if half is missing."

Dr. Bak Nguyen

1515

"The quest for happiness, as well as the quest for
power both share a common treat. They are both
based on influence, not ownership."

Dr. Bak Nguyen

1516

"Fun is greatly augmented as it is shared.
It is there that fun will grow into magic."
Dr. Bak Nguyen

1517

FROM THE POWER BEHIND THE ALPHA

"Happiness will make everything look easier
and will embellish everything we touch."
Dr. Bak Nguyen

1518

FROM THE POWER BEHIND THE ALPHA

" Happiness is the state of mind where no matter
where you choose to go, you are excited
and at peace at the same time."
Dr. Bak Nguyen

1519

FROM THE POWER BEHIND THE ALPHA

"Happiness is the opportunity to open up
and to share, every day."
Dr. Bak Nguyen

1520

"Happiness leads to generosity
and generosity, to abundance."

Dr. Bak Nguyen

1521

" HAPPINESS - RESPECT - HUMILITY - FORGIVENESS"

Dr. Bak Nguyen

1522

FROM HYBRID

"For a chance to happiness and to real worth,
one cannot simply overwrite his identity,
what nature intended for him."

Dr. Bak Nguyen

1523

FROM HYBRID

"To feel and to play are contagious."

Dr. Bak Nguyen

1524

FROM REBOOT, TO GROW FROM MIDLIFE CRISIS

"Happiness is the responsibility of one,
and only oneself."

Dr. Bak Nguyen

1525

FROM REBOOT, TO GROW FROM MIDLIFE CRISIS

"To be happy, one must be whole."

Dr. Bak Nguyen

1526

FROM FORCES OF NATURE

"You will never erase that smile on my face
nor the light of joy and hope in my heart. "

Dr. Bak Nguyen

1527

FROM FORCES OF NATURE

"Happiness isn't from the laugh
but the lift of the weight."

Dr. Bak Nguyen

1528
FROM SELFMADE
"To force a situation has never been the
key to any happiness."
Dr. Bak Nguyen

1529
FROM THE RISE OF THE UNICORN
"Happiness is a primal state of mind,
those were the wings of the angels."
Dr. Bak Nguyen

1530
FROM THE RISE OF THE UNICORN
"When no one was there,
eHappyPedia was there with me."
Dr. Bak Nguyen

1531
FROM THE RISE OF THE UNICORN
"eHappyPedia is exactly that, to share and to enjoy."
Dr. Bak Nguyen

1532
FROM MIRRORS
"To be whole is the only way to happiness."
Dr. Bak Nguyen

1533

FROM THE RISE OF THE UNICORN

"When one feels unhappy, don't complain,
keep pushing until the weather, the environment,
even time have changed. And then, keep pushing!"
Dr. Bak Nguyen

1534

FROM CHAMPION MINDSET

"I finally succeed to aligned my NARRATIVE and
my IDENTITY, that's how I found my happiness."
Dr. Bak Nguyen

1535

FROM POWER, EMOTIONAL INTELLIGENCE

"We make our happiness!"
Dr. Bak Nguyen

1536

FROM HORIZON VOLUME ONE

"There were simply excuses for me to find back
the joy and magic of my childhood."
Dr. Bak Nguyen

1537

FROM THE POWER OF YES VOLUME 3

"Everyone is looking to be happy, right?"

Dr. Bak Nguyen

1538

FROM HOW TO NOT FAIL AS A DENTIST

"To be free and a chance to be happy,
get your math right!"

Dr. Bak Nguyen

1539

FROM HOW TO NOT FAIL AS A DENTIST

"Value being more than having, that's your way
to freedom, happiness and… assets."

Dr. Bak Nguyen

1540

FROM MINDSET ARMORY

"To compare cannot bring you to
any happy ending, ever."

Dr. Bak Nguyen

1541

FROM MINDSET ARMORY

"To be content is not to be happy, but not at all."

Dr. Bak Nguyen

1542

FROM MASTERMIND

"Happiness is worth it. Power has too many liabilities attached to it."

Dr. Bak Nguyen

1543

FROM PLAYBOOK INTRODUCTION VOLUME 1

"Writing will bring happiness to anyone. Therefore, writing can change the world."

Dr. Bak Nguyen

1544

FROM PLAYBOOK INTRODUCTION VOLUME 1

"Actually, the less weight, the happier."

Dr. Bak Nguyen

1545

FROM SUCCESS IS A CHOICE

"Expect departures and separations to happen our your way to freedom. Not everyone is looking to be free!"

Dr. Bak Nguyen

1546

FROM THE 90 DAYS CHALLENGE

"Cooking was my way of be grateful and positive, about food."

Dr. Bak Nguyen

1547

FROM RISING

"It is easier to show the way to wealth
than it is to happiness."
Dr. Bak Nguyen

1548

FROM RISING

"Freedom is the absence of control, so is happiness."
Dr. Bak Nguyen

1549

FROM MIDAS TOUCH

"Smile and the world will be yours!"
Dr. Bak Nguyen

1550

FROM MIDAS TOUCH

"True beauty blossoms from profound happiness!"
Dr. Bak Nguyen

1551

FROM BOOTCAMP

"Look for happiness, share happiness, deliver
happiness. Success is the next stop."
Dr. Bak Nguyen

1552

FROM TOUCHSTONE, LEVERAGING TODAY'S PSYCHOLOGICAL SMOG

"Emptiness is not a void, but the absence of worries, of interests. Somehow, we came to fear that emptiness as a void of life."

Dr. Bak Nguyen

1553

FROM THE RISE OF THE UNICORN VOLUME TWO

"From Happiness, I changed my tagline to healing and to growing instead."

Dr. Bak Nguyen

1554

FROM THE RISE OF THE UNICORN VOLUME TWO

"Happiness is your own business and vision. To each our own happiness."

Dr. Bak Nguyen

1555

FROM THE RISE OF THE UNICORN VOLUME TWO

"This is my happiness, to have enough time to leverage my failures into successes."

Dr. Bak Nguyen

1556

FROM MIRRORS

"The only thing that we can have control upon is the pace of our own evolution."

Dr. Bak Nguyen

This is **Shortcut volume 7, Happiness**. Welcome to the Alphas.

Smile, that's the C major chord of the ballade.

Dr. BAK NGUYEN

PART 3
"LOVE"
by Dr. BAK NGUYEN

Love, I won't waste your time telling you what is love. What I will share with you is what love did for me. First, as a child, I received much love, not only from my parents but from my grandparents, and my uncles and aunts.

Then, I learnt more about love as I became a big brother and gave love. I experienced and quickly, I learnt to give and gave. It is easy to love those who love you. Giving love hoping, that is another story.

The family construct of love shaped most of my childhood and teenager's years, loving and protecting. That's what I knew, that's what I gave. Well, if loving is great, protecting is not as simple.

With the notion of protection, we imply that we are stronger, smarter and the loved party is weaker, smaller even stupid. This is why **loving protecting** can only go so far… eventually, it becomes insulting.

Even worse, what about our limitations and own boundaries. It is an insult as the younger party grow. But what about the other side of the comparison, us? Are we still stronger, wiser? What about our own handicaps and blindsides?

So just like most families, we grew apart with most bitterness, transforming love into hate, good intentions into pressure, and wounds.

Then, I found another kind of love, love with a capital L. I married that Love and healed from the warmth of its embraces. This time, there was no protection side, just to have someone to trust and to give to, without holding back. As I gave, I received even more.

I am a Force of Nature. Even if my family forged me to be stable, solid as a rock, my nature is shapeless. My force comes and goes with my moods, or with the winds as my father will say. Well, finding true Love, Tranie was the ground and the mountain on which I could lay and sleep.

I saw that very clearly as I travelled from continental Canada to Vancouver Island. On the Pacific, there are thousands of Islands. On each island stands a mountain. This is how grandiose and unique Canadian nature is.

Well, I also notice that in the sky, the clouds were only forming on top of these mountains. Except for the cloud in very high altitude, the cirrus, cirrocumulus, and cirrostratus class, the sky was clear and the clouds were companions of the mountains.

Well, that was the reflection of my couple: Tranie is the mountain and I was the cloud. For all those who know me, no one will ever believe that I would have pronounced these words. I was raised as a pillar, a proud gentleman, and a provider… and now, I say that I am shapeless and I need a mountain to rest, to lay.

Well, this is the damage **protection** did to me. Strap down a cloud and make it into a mountain. Not only you will have to attach the limps strongly, but you will also have to inject much weight to keep the cloud from floating. Then, as it might show some results, you will need to clip more and more of its attribute to keep it down. This is how I got my wings amputated.

Love was their excuse and love was my reason to submit myself to such treatment. I did not rebel because these were the people I love the most and they taught me everything I knew about love. Did they?

Well, until I met Tranie, that was all I knew about love. Meeting Tranie and loving her, making love to her, she unstrained the anchors and freed my true nature. She let me be and I healed.

Then, as I spent more and more time with her, the weight injections to keep me down to earth were getting more and more out-of-date and they slowly fade away. Most of my anchors evaporated with time. Those that were not, well, my transformation and ascension back as a cloud frightened them so much that they cut themselves from me, liberating me of all of my anchors.

Today, I am what Nature intended for me, a cloud. I can turn into a storm, rain, and swallow an entire mountain if I am angry. I can also provide the rain and the fertility to those looking for fresh water and some freshness.

I healed thanks to the love and generosity of Tranie, the ground, the mountain as the base of my family. From her love, I grew and became more powerful, assumed more shapes and since I have so much freedom, I could also be kind and generous without threatening my own existence.

Actually, the Love she showed me, allowed me to discover the secret of growth, from generosity. Whoever is growing and changing shape will tell you how unsecured and vulnerable we feel in such a situation. Well, Tranie's love provided the warmth and security I needed before I fuelled my **Confidence** fully.

I will say that I owe her my happiness and my powers, without her love, I will still be looking at my anchors, not knowing what to do and clouding my happiness at its source. No one can be happy mutes, amputated and cut from half of him or herself. This is what I called healing from **Conformity** and this is how we are all connected:

"We all need healing."
Dr. Bak Nguyen

That was the beginning of our journey of **SHORTCUT**, healing. The universal language of love is when someone is giving. That's unconditional love. In some cultures, that's also called sacrifice. Without replenishment, that kind of love has, by design, an expiration date.

I've been loved. Thanks to my status as a big brother, I learnt quickly, very early on, to give too. I received love from those above me and I gave love to those younger than me, not to say below me. But that is really what it was, a hierarchy system of love, with people above and people below.

Tranie's love changed all of that. There was no above or below. I received love and that was it. Then, as I loved in

51

return, I was even more grateful to have someone to **spoil** and to share with. Our love made us into partners and equals.

We do not have the same ambitions, needs nor even desires. We are often standing on opposite sides of most of life's issues. Thanks to that difference, I open my heart and my mind to the other half of life inaccessible to me until that point. Her love showed me an entirely new universe. Just as my love unlocked a world of possibilities to her.

We hold each other hands and discover the new and revisit the old as friends, as lovers, as equals. And this is the underline story that you will be reading about underneath each of the quotes and journey about love.

I loved and I found happiness.

This is **Shortcut volume 7, Happiness**. Welcome to the Alphas.

Dr. BAK NGUYEN

PART 4

"62 LOVE QUOTES"

by Dr. BAK NGUYEN

1741

FROM SYMPHONY OF SKILLS

"Love is the wind to your wings and
the safe ground for your landing"

Dr. Bak Nguyen

1742

FROM SYMPHONY OF SKILLS

"It is not because a first heart was easy to get that
I will find another one ... even after multiple efforts."

Dr. Bak Nguyen

1743

FROM SYMPHONY OF SKILLS

"Balance momentum from body to mind
and mind to body. it might save the world!"

Dr. Bak Nguyen

1744

FROM LEADERSHIP, PANDORA'S BOX

"To be generous is to love, ourself, and others."

Dr. Bak Nguyen

1745
FROM LEADERSHIP, PANDORA'S BOX
" To love is to respect one's right to find out more of oneself. To care is to be there when one's require an opened heart to share with."
Dr. Bak Nguyen

1746
FROM LEADERSHIP, PANDORA'S BOX
"Without Love, Life is colourless and Time is a burden."
Dr. Bak Nguyen

1747
FROM LEADERSHIP, PANDORA'S BOX
"Love is a feeling. It possesses us. We do not possess love. Be warned."
Dr. Bak Nguyen

1748
FROM IDENTITY, ANTHOLOGY OF QUESTS
"Music is universal, so is love and so is life."
Dr. Bak Nguyen

1749

FROM IDENTITY, ANTHOLOGY OF QUESTS

"Sing and you'll be making love with you soul!"

Dr. Bak Nguyen

1750

FROM IDENTITY, ANTHOLOGY OF QUESTS

"The power of love is within the awakening of one's soul to the possibilities of a merge, a synergy."

Dr. Bak Nguyen

1751

FROM IDENTITY, ANTHOLOGY OF QUESTS

"Love is the first and kindest teacher since it doesn't aim to protect but rather to prepare."

Dr. Bak Nguyen

1752

FROM INDUSTRIES' DISRUPTORS

"Those misguided attachments change the lightness of love into a burden."

Dr. Bak Nguyen

1753

"Forged in LOVE with the heat of TIME,
the mastery is the Alpha."

Dr. Bak Nguyen

1754

" To love without pride, without leverage."

Tranie Vo & Dr. Bak Nguyen

1755

" In our couple, the dynamic of control is a ball
that we pass around."

Dr. Bak Nguyen

1756

" I let go of perfection and control to embrace trust
and respect. That's the momentum of love."

Dr. Bak Nguyen

1757
" Our LOVE is dynamic and organic,
a natural flow of energy."
Dr. Bak Nguyen

1758
" My confidence groomed from love, in other words,
my own personal identity, is the best shield for my
LOVE and my couple's identity. "
Dr. Bak Nguyen

1759
" Love taught me respect, not perfection."
Dr. Bak Nguyen

1760
" From love, happiness. From happiness,
a life of success."
Dr. Bak Nguyen

1761

" The love of a power woman allowed me to grow faster since I let the burden of resistance behind."

Dr. Bak Nguyen

1762

" I am not complete without the love of my power woman, nor am I powerful."

Dr. Bak Nguyen

1763

"The first power woman in my life, the first power couple I knew. Back then, I simply called them happy."

Dr. Bak Nguyen

1764

" From the love of a power woman, we build with synergy. From an Alpha woman, we build from the force of the WILL."

Dr. Bak Nguyen

1765

"Love is the energy feeding greatness."

Dr. Bak Nguyen

1766

"Happiness, that's the source
of the unlimited power of the Alpha."

Dr. Bak Nguyen

1767

"From now on, this is the way that I'll be expressing
my love, by emptying myself to feel her vibe,
her desires, her nuances."

Dr. Bak Nguyen

1768

"The recipe of love is found more in the journey
than in the outcome."

Dr. Bak Nguyen

1769

FROM THE POWER BEHIND THE ALPHA

"Facing the unknown, she was the element
I knew best. Even if we had just met..."

Dr. Bak Nguyen

1770

FROM THE POWER BEHIND THE ALPHA

" Love shouldn't be about sacrifice,
but empowerment."

Dr. Bak Nguyen

1771

FROM THE POWER BEHIND THE ALPHA

"In love, you do not need your mind as a burden.
Just an open heart."

Dr. Bak Nguyen

1772

FROM THE POWER BEHIND THE ALPHA

"LOVE and BELIEF made her whole,
the lack of doubt made it easier."

Dr. Bak Nguyen

1773

"The shift of gears is what made us
into a power couple."

Dr. Bak Nguyen

1774

" It was confusing to be forging in the name of love
and inspired with love."

Dr. Bak Nguyen

1775

"To love a story, pay attention.
To understand one, listen to the underscore."

Dr. Bak Nguyen

1776

"Nothing feels more grateful than
to have the chance to touch a life for the better. "

Dr. Bak Nguyen

1777

FROM REBOOT, TO GROW FROM MIDLIFE CRISIS

"Their Love grew slowly to replace Desire.
And he went with the flow,
embracing love and its growth."
Dr. Bak Nguyen

1778

FROM REBOOT, TO GROW FROM MIDLIFE CRISIS

"Love and Sex are two completely different things!"
Dr. Bak Nguyen

1779

FROM REBOOT, TO GROW FROM MIDLIFE CRISIS

"A hope for Love, for Fulfilment, for Happiness."
Dr. Bak Nguyen

1780

FROM REBOOT, TO GROW FROM MIDLIFE CRISIS

"The key to personal happiness is acceptance
and empowerment."
Dr. Bak Nguyen

1781

FROM REBOOT, TO GROW FROM MIDLIFE CRISIS

"In the name of Love, of God and of Happiness,
we must do better."

Dr. Bak Nguyen

1782

FROM FORCES OF NATURE

"Love comes in all sauces, sometimes,
wrapped with bitterness and nostalgia."

Dr. Bak Nguyen

1783

FROM FORCES OF NATURE

"To all the women in my life, past, present, and future,
you are light and love all at once."

Dr. Bak Nguyen

1784

FROM HOW TO WRITE A BOOK IN 30 DAYS

"The dialogue was the beginning. From there,
you can build a relationship, even a love story!"

Dr. Bak Nguyen

1785

FROM HORIZON VOLUME ONE

"I love Tranie, and I am built to please whom I love."

Dr. Bak Nguyen

1786

FROM MINDSET ARMORY

"Giving me three gifts, she gave me the entirety of her love and hope."

Dr. Bak Nguyen

1787

FROM HORIZON VOLUME THREE

"Love helped me to unburden myself to heal…"

Dr. Bak Nguyen

1788

FROM HORIZON VOLUME THREE

"Tranie, I love you. By your side, Past and Future blend into Present. A present wrapped with kindness and style."

Dr. Bak Nguyen

1789

FROM EMPOWERMENT

"If nothing is impossible with THE POWER OF HOPE, nothing heals better than THE POWER OF LOVE."

Dr. Bak Nguyen

1790

"The seed of hope is the maternal love we received."

Dr. Bak Nguyen

1791

FROM THE MODERN WOMAN

"…and the guardian of that sacred fire
is within the woman's heart."

Dr. Bak Nguyen

1792

FROM THE MODERN WOMAN

"Mother Nature lives within each of your breath.
Aphrodite charms within each of your smile."

Dr. Bak Nguyen

1793

FROM THE UAX STORY

"A woman heart is much bigger in size than a man's."

Dr. Bak Nguyen

1794

FROM 1SELF

"Attention is not love, as attention can only be
divided, love can be multiplied."

Dr. Bak Nguyen

1795

FROM MIRRORS

"A moment is a pocket where time loses its grip, a window where the burden is lifted, and the feeling of lightness and freedom are the only ambiances. "
Dr. Bak Nguyen

1796

FROM MIRRORS

"The minute the watch ticks louder than the heart, the moment is gone."
Dr. Bak Nguyen

1797

FROM MIRRORS

"Love can be felt, lived, touched, tasted and to keep it alive, have to come back knocking every day."
Dr. Bak Nguyen

1798

FROM TO OVERACHIEVE EVERYTHING BEING LAZY

"If you were looking for love with a capital L, well, attraction is a far better way (laziness wise) to active seeking!"
Dr. Bak Nguyen

1799

FROM TO OVERACHIEVE EVERYTHING BEING LAZY

"Loving is about giving and growth."

Dr. Bak Nguyen

1800

FROM TO OVERACHIEVE EVERYTHING BEING LAZY

"To every attempt of gratitude, my love was put
to the test, until I stopped sharing and started giving."

Dr. Bak Nguyen

1801

FROM TO OVERACHIEVE EVERYTHING BEING LAZY

"As for me, love is to give. To have people to give to
is the most precious of gifts."

Dr. Bak Nguyen

1802

FROM TO OVERACHIEVE EVERYTHING BEING LAZY

"Keep in mine that relationships are a two-way streets.
Whatever is one-way, is either short terms or a lie."

Dr. Bak Nguyen

This is **Shortcut volume 7, Happiness**. Welcome to the Alphas.

Smile, that's the C major chord of the ballade.

Dr. BAK NGUYEN

PART 5

"PARENTING"

by Dr. BAK NGUYEN

If **Love** with a capital L allowed me to heal and to start my rise, I founded another kind of love that propelled me to new heights. And that is the love of a father, from the giving end.

I love Tranie with all of my heart and that's why I kneeled down and proposed to her, seven years after first kissing her. I was ready to share my life with her but I was not ready to share neither her nor my life with anyone else!

After the wedding, actually, people did not even wait until the end of the celebrations to ask about when will we be having our first baby!!! That killed most of my libido!

I heard once a saying that will be haunting me for years: "We spent our lives fighting to become number 1 and suddenly, we become number 2 and we are happy about it." Well, I was stuck as a dentist, far from my aspirations of Hollywood and Wall Street, I wasn't ready to simply cap and to take care of a child!

On plans, I bought a condo on the last floor of a brand new building complex. I had 2 bedrooms and I blew out one to postpone the eventuality of becoming a dad as far as possible. My friends all told me how stupid I was, losing 15% of the value of my condo but I did not care.

Instead, I had one of the most luxurious hotel lounges to be my corner of paradise. This is how fanatic I was about fatherhood. Well, my son arrived 5 years later.

During the last 5 years, I was successful and on cruise control. I left my ambitions and aspirations aside (for 10 years) and focus on being the best dentist I could be. I was prosperous, loved, and respected.

I was busy and forgot about my ambitions… until the **checkpoints** arrived. Becoming a dad was one of these **checkpoints**. A baby is a baby, it cries, eats, sleeps, and poops. You, you hold, feed, take pictures, and clean. That's the game, one the is no break nor return policy.

From being the centre of attention of my wife, I was now at the bottom of… everything. There was the baby and its needs, the mothers, all the layers of craps possible and I was at the bottom, feeding and providing. No sex nor empowerment either!

And on top of that, I could not say a word to anyone, including myself. What kind of loser will complain about being a father? I muted myself and went with the flow.

But then, something magical happened. I have the night shift taking care of William. From 8 PM to 6 AM, that was my shift to allow Tranie to rest. To feed William before midnight was easy, it was within the night that it was more challenging.

So I learnt to play with him and to feed him and 8 PM. Then, I know that the next time that he will go hungry will be around 11:30 - 12 AM. Well, I stretched that to the maximum, sometimes going until 12:30 AM before feeding him. We played, even if he was hungry.

Then, by 12:30, as he is fed, the next time that he will be hungry again will be around 4 to 4:30 AM. That was okay with me since after feeding him, I will be ready to shower and to hit the road for the office anyway.

Well, for the first 6 months of William's life, I never saw as many sunrises in my entire life. From my hotel lounge, I had a clear view of the sun rising. One morning after the next, I had much time to think, looking at William sleeping in my arms once he was fed.

Well, I did not want to repeat the same mistakes that I saw from love and family. I did not want to break him nor to be the protection that he will despite eventually. So instead of teaching him to become stronger and smarter, I will teach him to be generous and flexible. Strength and intelligence, those I assumed that he is!

Also, I did not want to be a protector, not anymore. So instead of putting the **pressure of expectation** on him, I put those on myself. I will have to become what I would love him to become, Then, all he will have to do is to copy.

I went from praising strength and smart to become generous and flexible. Well, generosity was already part of my DNA. Being flexible, not so much! The years will pass before I will yield such power, but I did eventually. I grew because I was standing on the giving end.

William had a wonderful childhood, just like mine, surrounded by love from all sides. I did not raise him in religion and stayed away from most **Conformities**. To me, what was crucial was to let him grow his **Confidence**.

Then, my plan worked. He grew, copying me. He became quite smart, strong, generous, and flexible. At 5 years old, he taught me back, telling me to be **happy, happy, happy!** That's the story of **eHappyPedia**.

Then as I faced a cliff as a crossroad, going through my hormones, sexual desires and midlife crisis, William at 8 offered himself to refocus my energy. We made History together, breaking the **sound barrier** and writing world records, yes, records, with an s!

William grew much from that episode, because he too, learnt to give. He wrapped me with his love and innocence, and together, we discovered new powers. I went from writing **15 books in 15 months** to **36 books in 18 months + 1 week**! How did we write 21 books within 3 months and 1 week?

That happened from the love we shared. Since love occurs at the giving end, we were both giving so we both grew. On top of that, we were both sharing, so we also grew from the other's growth. We became the best of buddies.

From a man terrified to become a dad, I became the hero of both my story and William's, not as an underlink but as a partner, a co-author, a buddy!

Just as I discovered Love with a capital L, I found an **equal** and I grew from giving. I discovered a new level of energy and happiness as a father in parenting and looking to raise an equal. Actually, the right word is more *rise* than *raise*, even as father and son!

This is **Shortcut volume 7, Happiness**. Welcome to the Alphas.

Smile, that's the C major chord of the ballade.

Dr. BAK NGUYEN

PART 6
"86 PARENTING QUOTES"
by Dr. BAK NGUYEN

2178

FROM SYMPHONY OF SKILLS

"Be strong, be smart, be flexible,
be generous and be kind."

Dr. Bak Nguyen

2179

FROM LEADERSHIP, PANDORA'S BOX

"We were born little, but some will choose
to stay small. That's not the same."

Dr. Bak Nguyen

2180

FROM IDENTITY, ANTHOLOGY OF QUESTS

"Little and small aren't the same. We were all born
little. Some will choose to stay small while others, with
an opened heart and opened mind will grow."

Dr. Bak Nguyen

2181

FROM IDENTITY, ANTHOLOGY OF QUESTS

"Little is a privilege to be enjoyed fully while it lasts.
We called it childhood."

Dr. Bak Nguyen

2182

FROM IDENTITY, ANTHOLOGY OF QUESTS

"Let go of what you know. The egg shell that was our shield will not protect us from much."

Dr. Bak Nguyen

2183

FROM IDENTITY, ANTHOLOGY OF QUESTS

"Powerful is a lion that can fly!
We call those the dragon hearts!"

Dr. Bak Nguyen

2184

FROM IDENTITY, ANTHOLOGY OF QUESTS

"You want to prepare, not to protect."

Dr. Bak Nguyen

2185

FROM REBOOT, TO GROW FROM MIDLIFE CRISIS

"No sex, no praise, no empowerment.
But he is now a dad!"

Dr. Bak Nguyen

2186

FROM THE BOOK OF LEGENDS, VOLUME 1

"Sometimes, I am more of a big brother
to my son than a dad..."

Dr. Bak Nguyen

2187

FROM THE BOOK OF LEGENDS, VOLUME 1

"Easy and fun were the keys."

Dr. Bak Nguyen

2188

FROM THE BOOK OF LEGENDS, VOLUME 1

"I am pretty aware of the importance of Confidence
in a kid's development, of self-confidence."

Dr. Bak Nguyen

2189

FROM THE BOOK OF LEGENDS, VOLUME 1

"Whatever you want to teach your kids, do it first.
Master it and they will follow your example."

Dr. Bak Nguyen

2190

FROM THE BOOK OF LEGENDS, VOLUME 1

"What makes a Lion is his heart."

Dr. Bak Nguyen

2524

FROM THE BOOK OF LEGENDS, VOLUME 1

"Where do we draw the line between abundance and spoil?"

Dr. Bak Nguyen

2191

FROM THE BOOK OF LEGENDS, VOLUME 1

"As a dad, you find Will you didn't know you had in you..."

Dr. Bak Nguyen

2192

FROM THE BOOK OF LEGENDS, VOLUME 1

"I will not expect anything. I will do and hope. Worst case scenario, I will have been."

Dr. Bak Nguyen

2193

FROM THE BOOK OF LEGENDS, VOLUME 1

"I was steel. I knew fire. It was time for me to combine the two of them. Will and love."

Dr. Bak Nguyen

2194

FROM THE BOOK OF LEGENDS, VOLUME 1

"Be strong, be smart, be kind, be generous
and be flexible. To that, he added, be happy."

Dr. Bak Nguyen and William Bak

2195

FROM THE BOOK OF LEGENDS, VOLUME 1

"The warmth of love opened my heart
to accept the teaching of a kid."

Dr. Bak Nguyen

2196

FROM THE BOOK OF LEGENDS, VOLUME 1

"I love, I believe and I bet on myself."

Dr. Bak Nguyen

2197

FROM THE BOOK OF LEGENDS, VOLUME 1

"I have become a better father and a better person
since I now let my feelings sink in first."

Dr. Bak Nguyen

2198

FROM THE BOOK OF LEGENDS, VOLUME 1

"Confidence is my priority. His confidence."

Dr. Bak Nguyen

2199

FROM THE BOOK OF LEGENDS, VOLUME 1

"Be the difference you want to make.
That's the only way to grow honestly."

Dr. Bak Nguyen

2200

FROM THE BOOK OF LEGENDS, VOLUME 1

"I gave into it without holding back, empowering
William to speak with confidence. "

Dr. Bak Nguyen

2201

FROM THE BOOK OF LEGENDS, VOLUME 1

"Invisible and flexible were the smash up
of our geniuses."

Dr. Bak Nguyen and William Bak

2202

FROM THE BOOK OF LEGENDS, VOLUME 1

"If anything, William gave me my wings, as a dragon."

Dr. Bak Nguyen

2203

FROM THE BOOK OF LEGENDS, VOLUME 1

"Be careful what you wish for, especially around me!"

Dr. Bak Nguyen

2204
FROM THE BOOK OF LEGENDS, VOLUME 1
"But honey, the kid is right,
it would be a great statement to make!"
Dr. Bak Nguyen

2205
FROM THE BOOK OF LEGENDS, VOLUME 1
"To give him infinity and a world record,
that would be a hell of a Christmas gift!"
Dr. Bak Nguyen

2206
FROM THE BOOK OF LEGENDS, VOLUME 1
"I may not fly, but I might last forever,
for as long as my purpose serves the many."
Dr. Bak Nguyen

2207
FROM THE BOOK OF LEGENDS, VOLUME 1
"I gave him the endless sense of possibilities."
Dr. Bak Nguyen

2208
FROM THE BOOK OF LEGENDS, VOLUME 1
"Hope and fear are siblings that can be very similar."
Dr. Bak Nguyen

2209
FROM THE BOOK OF LEGENDS, VOLUME 1
"What to expect from the unexpected?
To be able to embrace gracefully."
Dr. Bak Nguyen

2210
FROM THE BOOK OF LEGENDS, VOLUME 1
"Love and fatherhood fixed and improved
most of my systems and core beliefs."
Dr. Bak Nguyen

2211
FROM SELFMADE
"Flexibility and generosity will be my gift to William."
Dr. Bak Nguyen

2212
FROM SELFMADE
"My child empowered my values and my evolution."
Dr. Bak Nguyen

2213
FROM SELFMADE
"To have a chance with your kid, make it into a game.
You might like it too!"
Dr. Bak Nguyen

2214

FROM SELFMADE

"You can't force evolution, you can only empower it."
Dr. Bak Nguyen

2215

FROM THE BOOK OF LEGENDS, VOLUME 2

"I am not pushing him, he is pushing me!"
Dr. Bak Nguyen

2216

FROM THE BOOK OF LEGENDS, VOLUME 2

"Merit, when deserved, is very powerful."
Dr. Bak Nguyen

2217

FROM THE BOOK OF LEGENDS, VOLUME 2

"The warnings are everywhere. If only one opens
his eyes to see, and his heart to understand."
Dr. Bak Nguyen

2218

FROM THE BOOK OF LEGENDS, VOLUME 2

"A SUPER CHICKEN, I am no more!"
Dr. Bak Nguyen

2219

FROM THE BOOK OF LEGENDS, VOLUME 2

"We are uncovering superpowers and their meaning
as we keep our connections and discovering the
world through the stories of Chickens."
Dr. Bak Nguyen

2220

FROM THE BOOK OF LEGENDS, VOLUME 2

"Skill are intelligence and strength.
Powerful are Gratitude and Kindness."
Dr. Bak Nguyen

2221

FROM THE BOOK OF LEGENDS, VOLUME 2

"If you want to know the mindset of a rich person,
look at the way he is training his kids."
Dr. Bak Nguyen

2222

FROM THE BOOK OF LEGENDS, VOLUME 2

"Be careful of what you wish for,
especially around me."
Dr. Bak Nguyen

2223

FROM THE BOOK OF LEGENDS, VOLUME 2

"Open yourself up to your kids.
You'll be surprised how amazing their minds work."
Dr. Bak Nguyen

2224

FROM THE BOOK OF LEGENDS, VOLUME 2

"Faith and resilience will polish any trait
into a power, a superpower."
Dr. Bak Nguyen

2225

FROM THE BOOK OF LEGENDS, VOLUME 2

"Hope is the word, Hope is the matrix,
Hope is the power."
Dr. Bak Nguyen

2226

FROM THE BOOK OF LEGENDS, VOLUME 2

"Life as usual… writing books and keep pushing
further and further the world record."
Dr. Bak Nguyen

2227

FROM THE BOOK OF LEGENDS, VOLUME 2

"Every time we help someone, it is a chance to learn and to grow ourselves."

Dr. Bak Nguyen

2228

FROM THE BOOK OF LEGENDS, VOLUME 2

"By keeping a tension, you create a void that Nature likes to fill."

Dr. Bak Nguyen

2229

FROM THE BOOK OF LEGENDS, VOLUME 2

"Keep your word to keep your heart open."

Dr. Bak Nguyen

2230

FROM THE BOOK OF LEGENDS, VOLUME 2

"Something really bad happens each time you lie."

Dr. Bak Nguyen

2231

FROM THE BOOK OF LEGENDS, VOLUME 2

"It takes courage to admit that you were wrong."

Dr. Bak Nguyen

2232

FROM THE BOOK OF LEGENDS, VOLUME 2

"Being ungrateful is more than just forgetting
to say please and thank you…"

Dr. Bak Nguyen

2233

FROM THE BOOK OF LEGENDS, VOLUME 2

"Do not talk about something or someone
until you've tried his shoes and tasted his food!"

Dr. Bak Nguyen

2234

FROM THE BOOK OF LEGENDS, VOLUME 2

"The worst attitude is to not know and not learn."

Dr. Bak Nguyen

2235

FROM THE BOOK OF LEGENDS, VOLUME 2

"It's never okay to hurt someone on purpose.
No matter how you put it."

Dr. Bak Nguyen

2236

FROM THE BOOK OF LEGENDS, VOLUME 2

"Have people laugh with you, about you, not of you!"

Dr. Bak Nguyen

2237

FROM THE BOOK OF LEGENDS, VOLUME 2

"You have no idea how strong, smart and powerful
you'll be growing by helping and sharing."

Dr. Bak Nguyen

2238

FROM THE BOOK OF LEGENDS, VOLUME 2

"When you hear people telling you to listen
to your inner voice, start listening
to your outspoken words first."

Dr. Bak Nguyen

2239

FROM THE BOOK OF LEGENDS, VOLUME 2

"That's why I don't scream louder than I think
since I need to hear myself thinking."

Dr. Bak Nguyen

2240

FROM THE BOOK OF LEGENDS, VOLUME 2

"Gently and kindly are the keys to much of the world."

Dr. Bak Nguyen

2241
FROM THE BOOK OF LEGENDS, VOLUME 2
"When you laugh, that helps
to keep your heart open."
Dr. Bak Nguyen

2242
FROM THE BOOK OF LEGENDS, VOLUME 2
"Embrace the day and face the sun, that's the only
way to face the day and the challenges ahead."
Dr. Bak Nguyen

2243
FROM THE BOOK OF LEGENDS, VOLUME 2
"And where there is no solution, make one up!
You are already in trouble anyway,
what do you have to lose?"
Dr. Bak Nguyen

2244
FROM THE BOOK OF LEGENDS, VOLUME 2
"If we assume the parallel between FLYING and
DREAMING, I could make chickens fly… eventually."
Dr. Bak Nguyen

2245

FROM THE BOOK OF LEGENDS, VOLUME 2

"To keep your MOMENTUM growing, feed it a win.
As small as it is, feed it a win, ASAP!"

Dr. Bak Nguyen

2246

FROM THE BOOK OF LEGENDS, VOLUME 2

"The power of the universe is in your heart.
Find it and free it."

Dr. Bak Nguyen

2247

FROM THE BOOK OF LEGENDS, VOLUME 2

"To dream is to feel and to let go."

Dr. Bak Nguyen

2248

FROM THE BOOK OF LEGENDS, VOLUME 2

"The kinder the heart, the bigger the dream."

Dr. Bak Nguyen

2249

FROM THE BOOK OF LEGENDS, VOLUME 2

"To dream, you've learnt to walk alone.
To grow your dream, now you must learn to share."

Dr. Bak Nguyen

2250
FROM THE BOOK OF LEGENDS, VOLUME 2
"To dream is to feel."
Dr. Bak Nguyen

2251
FROM THE BOOK OF LEGENDS, VOLUME 2
"It was all out of love, but now it was out of control."
Dr. Bak Nguyen

2252
FROM THE BOOK OF LEGENDS, VOLUME 2
"Fatherhood, I didn't know. I learnt reacting, kindly."
Dr. Bak Nguyen

2253
FROM BRANDING
"Let it out. Good or bad, let it out!"
Dr. Bak Nguyen & William Bak

2254
FROM HORIZON VOLUME ONE
"I love kids, I am a kid. I can relate."
Dr. Bak Nguyen

2255
FROM THE ENERGY FORMULA

"Only from the the love of a father, I could see clearly the assets from the liabilities."

Dr. Bak Nguyen

2256
FROM TOUCHSTONE, LEVERAGING TODAY'S PSYCHOLOGICAL SMOG

"The day I became a father, most of my fears faded away. I had too much to do to be fearful."

Dr. Bak Nguyen

2257
FROM THE VACCINE

"There are no stupid questions. Just stupid answers."

Dr. Bak Nguyen

2258
FROM 1SELF

"The love for my son melted the glass ceiling."

Dr. Bak Nguyen

2259
FROM THE BOOK OF LEGENDS VOLUME 3

"Everyone can be a hero, an ally, a mentor… and perhaps, even a dark hero."

Dr. Bak Nguyen

2260

FROM THE BOOK OF LEGENDS VOLUME 3

"The magic of innocence without expectation..."

Dr. Bak Nguyen

2261

FROM THE BOOK OF LEGENDS VOLUME 3

"Just like you can't force love,
no one can force magic."

Dr. Bak Nguyen

2262

FROM THE BOOK OF LEGENDS VOLUME 3

"As a father is looking to protect his kid,
a mentor is looking to empower his protege."

Dr. Bak Nguyen

2263

FROM THE BOOK OF LEGENDS VOLUME 3

"You can't force creativity. All you can do is
to empower it as it comes and react to it."

Dr. Bak Nguyen

This is **Shortcut volume 7, Happiness**. Welcome to the Alphas.

Smile, that's the C major chord of the ballade.

Dr. BAK NGUYEN

PART 7
"TRAVELLING"
by Dr. BAK NGUYEN

Travelling is another way to supercharge your growth and journey. Sure, most of the time travelling will rime with pleasure, vacations, and happiness. But much more than that, travelling is the quickest way to open or to keep your mind open.

Have you noticed that as you travel, all your senses are open and hypersensitive, at least for a little while? You noticed everything, you smell everything, you heard more and most of what surrounds you, and even your touch is aroused.

All of that is from the novelty effect, as you a moving into an unknown environment. What is arousing your sense can be fear, but most of the time, it will be curiosity and the feeling of unsettlement.

This feeling and the supercharging of your sense will last for a few days until you get familiarize with your new environment and eventually, your senses will be returning to their normal baseline.

But what did we learn so far, about our body, our hormones, and our minds? That the body produced hormones to which we will react. And the mind? Well, the mind is always slow to join the party, any party.

So what happens as you travel? True, for the first few days, your senses are aroused. That will kick your body producing hormones, much more hormones and surely different from those you had home, at your baseline.

Then, you are reacting to the increase of hormonal flux as you eating new spices and food. Sleeping in a different bed will also sustain yourself in a kind of dream-like state. So even after the awakening of your senses and its peak in arousal, you are still floating in a new bath of hormones and sensations.

This is usually when your mind will be joining the party. While every part of your body and senses are in an orgy of novelty and pleasure, your mind too will be joining, even reluctant. I am using here the sexual theme because it is a strong image, one that everyone can easily picture.

Well, your mind will be giving in, the conservative and strict, even uptight will be loosing up. For a little while, this is how you will set a new baseline to both your hormones and mind. Your senses will slowly have regained their baseline unless you keep changing environments.

Well, I told you that the mind is a slow player. As you are going back to your life, after that short episode of travelling, of living a different life, almost a dream, your body will keep producing the increased hormones for a little while and you will be reacting to those.

On top of that, your mind, as a slow player, will take some time before regressing to its baseline prior to travelling. That's your window of opportunity to go back at your life with a fresh perspective, an open mind.

Travelling is not my thing. I don't love travelling, I don't hate travelling either. I am simply too busy to think of travelling. On the other hand, Tranie lives to travel, to taste the spices, colours, and odours of the world.

For our first 5 years as newlywed couple, that is how I kept her happy, travelling and discovering the world as I spread out my continuous education hours across the globe. Loving her, I learn to love travelling and its effect on my mind.

Today, travelling and discovering is not only my chance to renew with my best friend and wife, looking to resume that lover's relationship we once shared, but it has become a standard of Life for William too!

We all felt the void in COVID times as travelling was difficult, not to say impossible. We felt and saw the effect of that void on our mental health, even physical health.

For the last 2 decades, I have struggled with my weight, this is no secret. Just prior to the COVID war, I successfully lost 16 pounds and was looking good, a first for years! I share that story in **THE 90 DAYS CHALLENGE**. Then COVID happened and after resisting for a few months, my body gave up.

I regained all of what I've lost and even doubled down on my weight. Almost a year later, I finally had the opportunity to travel again. Well, I went to Vancouver, the most remote and exotic place I could go without crossing any international frontier.

I went, had fun, and walk most of my days. I went from walking an average of 5000 steps a day to 20 000 + steps a day in vacation. Guess what? I gained 4 more pounds!

I was depressed. Sure, as we travelled, I ate and spoil my family with treats but nothing excessive to the point of gaining 4 more pounds on top of my double down results already! I went back home and moved on to write my world records.

I resumed my life, I did not change much of my eating habits. Within 10 days, I wrote and published 4 books, the first 4 **SHORTCUTS volumes** and I lost 8 pounds!

To write and publish a book every 2.5 days in a new height for me but that, I had my willpower to leverage on. But to lose 8 pounds, I had no idea of what happened... until I did.

I am still a doctor! I noticed that within the last 10 days, my urine was very dense and smelly. The 8 pounds that I lost was water, I was suffering from water retention. As my body purged itself for the extra electrolytes, hormones, and toxins that I have accumulated from the stress of COVID within the last 15 months, I rebalanced myself.

My mind needed that reset. As a result, I scored new world records trying to resume my trail. My body needed that reset. That, I never understood, until I felt the lift of the extra weight. Today, I am leveraging on that momentum to resume my regime and how I lost 16 pounds last year. By the time of this writing, I have lost 11 pounds during the last 30 days and I feel so good!

And this is a physical example of what it is to travel and its effect on our mind, hormones, and body.

We are fools to think that our body and mind are not linked. We are fools to think that our body is just a machine and that 8 hours of sleep a day are enough to replenish. It is about understanding what triggers our hormonal response and how to leverage on those.

Since we have a heavy tendency to close down and to be defensive, to hate change, and to defend the past, well, travelling twice a year should be mandatory, not to open your mind, but to keep an equilibrium between our habits and our health and state of mind. In other words, our life span and morale (happiness).

This is **Shortcut volume 7, Happiness**. Welcome to the Alphas.

Smile, that's the C major chord of the ballade.

Dr. BAK NGUYEN

PART 8
"24 TRAVELLING QUOTES"
by Dr. BAK NGUYEN

2357
FROM THE POWER BEHIND THE ALPHA
" Traveling is a quick fix to reboot our minds.
For a little while."
Dr. Bak Nguyen

2358
FROM MIRRORS
"Travelling is a great way to experience
the cheat of time."
Dr. Bak Nguyen

2359
FROM HORIZON VOLUME ONE
"When we travel, the colours are more intense,
the senses open and with or without our consent,
we are opening up. "
Dr. Bak Nguyen

2360
FROM HORIZON VOLUME ONE
"It was simply a magical time, year after year,
in the summer driving for weeks."
Dr. Bak Nguyen

2361

FROM HORIZON VOLUME ONE

"That day on the beach, I understood the meaning of thriving and its difference with surviving."

Dr. Bak Nguyen

2362

FROM HORIZON VOLUME ONE

"The journey is what makes the man, not the destination. The 101 was my journey to embrace my destiny."

Dr. Bak Nguyen

2363

FROM HORIZON VOLUME ONE

"Travelling in our hometown is surely something everyone should try. It is much revelling and empowering."

Dr. Bak Nguyen

2364

FROM HORIZON VOLUME ONE

"Give me a car and a GPS... and internet access and no matter where I am, I will be able to feel home."

Dr. Bak Nguyen

2365

FROM HORIZON VOLUME ONE
"It is something to read about history,
it is something else to walk history.
Only then, one can write history, wisely."
Dr. Bak Nguyen

2366

FROM HORIZON VOLUME ONE
"Travelling is the schooling from life, the fun part."
Dr. Bak Nguyen

2367

FROM HORIZON VOLUME ONE
"Creativity is a great way to expand one's mind,
even if he is stuck in one place. Travelling
is another way to expand one's mind."
Dr. Bak Nguyen

2368

FROM HORIZON VOLUME ONE
"We both want the same thing,
to expand our horizon, our family, our minds."
Dr. Bak Nguyen

2369
FROM HORIZON VOLUME TWO
"Travelling is not to stop, but to take
the time to replenish and to do things differently."

Dr. Bak Nguyen

2370
FROM HORIZON VOLUME TWO
"While travelling, our senses open up, naturally."

Dr. Bak Nguyen

2371
FROM HORIZON VOLUME TWO
"Travelling will keep your heart young."

Dr. Bak Nguyen

2372
FROM HORIZON VOLUME THREE
"Travelling opens eyes. Travelling opens mouths."

Dr. Bak Nguyen

2373
FROM HORIZON VOLUME THREE
"As we travel, we eat culture,
landscape and pleasure, literally."

Dr. Bak Nguyen

2374
FROM HORIZON VOLUME THREE
"For peace, for harmony for acceptance,
we need to travel more, right now."
Dr. Bak Nguyen

2375
FROM HORIZON VOLUME THREE
"Vegas is the permanent celebration of human
audacity and creative spirit."
Dr. Bak Nguyen

2376
FROM HORIZON VOLUME THREE
"LTE connection and Smartphone,
that's how we felt safe and free on foreign soil."
Dr. Bak Nguyen

2377
FROM HORIZON VOLUME THREE
"The world is such a big place.
Travel to see how little you are.
Drop your small EGO and start to grow."
Dr. Bak Nguyen

2378
FROM HORIZON VOLUME THREE

"I needed time and inspiration.
She needed space and inspiration.
We settled on inspiration giving each other
time and space."
Dr. Bak Nguyen

2379
FROM HORIZON VOLUME THREE

"TRAVELLING should be mandatory
within our educational journey."
Dr. Bak Nguyen

2380
FROM THE MODERN WOMAN

"To balance is to try hard to stand still."
Dr. Bak Nguyen

This is **Shortcut volume 7, Happiness**. Welcome to the Alphas.

Smile, that's the C major chord of the ballade.

Dr. BAK NGUYEN

PART 9

"THE POWER OF QUOTES"

by Dr. BAK NGUYEN

With this compilation of quotes, we are at the last volume of **SHORTCUT**. The next one, **DOCTOR** is more specific and will not be of general interest.

Before jumping back at the famous quotes, what did we learn so far? We learnt that we are in control. If we are aware and ready, we can leverage our emotions and feeling to empower our body and its hormones. As we feel, we will believe!

And how does one leverage his or her emotions? With the right mindset. That is what a quote is. It is either the mindset itself or the explanation of one. You use the mindsets (quotes) to stir your emotions or even to provoke them. Once your body has reacted, then, all you have to do is to surf the wave of hormones to propel yourself forward.

In society, we have been trained to do the exact opposite, to suppress and ignore our emotions, and then, as they burst, and they will, to do our best to contain them. First of all, doing so is suicide as you are keeping the grenade deep in your guts.

Secondly, what a waste of energy, from the burst, you are not harnessing any energy, on the contrary, you are spending even more energy to try to contain it! Can you see why you are stuck, even broken?

There is a safe way to release your emotions, we covered that in the first volume of **SHORTCUT, HEALING**. Be aware, be available, and know-how to express your emotions and to harness their power. That is what we did together, not only for the last 7 **SHORTCUT volumes** but since my debut with you, sharing quotes, anecdotes, and wisdom, 4 years ago.

This is the power of quotes, the power to change your Life. The power to show you where lays your power. And, by extension, it is the power to change the world, for the better, for more!

FAMOUS QUOTE 1

0012
FROM INDUSTRIES' DISRUPTORS
"Always choose the path of least resistance."
Dr. Bak Nguyen

This might seem a deep one, requiring much reflection. Well, I will be honest, it appeared to me in the heat of the moment. I was on stage, giving my first speaking event at the **JOHN MOLSON BUSINESS SCHOOL, CONCORDIA UNIVERSITY**.

I was on stage sharing my experience with a crowd of students and entrepreneurs when I urged people to be aware of the collaterals they are leaving on their trail. The conference was about industry disruptors and entrepreneurship.

I empowered the crowd to believe in themselves and their ideas.

> We are the change. We are proud of being that change because we see and we believe. But whatever new you are bringing to the table, it will be to replace an older one. There is where will come your resistance. Don't blind yourselves thinking that you have the right and only solution. Before acting, please be aware of the collaterals that you are causing. No plan is perfect but at least, if you are aware, you might encounter less resistance. At the end of the day, our goal was to help, no?

That was the essence of that speech. With any change, people will be opposing it unless the pain is much bigger than the pain of change. The pain of change and fear, there are your main enemies as you are looking to change the world, for the better.

In the context of a personal Quest of Identity, the same exact logic will apply. Only this time, the resistance is often parts of yourself or the people you keep the closest to your heart. Look and understand the **collaterals** and **resistance** will fade away.

As you are walking your legend, I told you that growth happens as you are serving others. Don't fool yourself, even those in need are fearful of change. Once more, identify the collaterals and you might be more skilled to avoid the cliffs and road bumps.

FAMOUS QUOTE 2

0022
FROM HYBRID
"Chords and patterns are the themes of the Universe."
Dr. Bak Nguyen

Well, I hope that by now, the idea of **energy** and of the **frequencies of the Universe**, you have accepted and understood. You don't have to believe me, you feel them all the time, you just need to be aware and to listen a little more.

Our emotions, we found a great way to canalize its energy and to communicate that from one person to the next. It is called music. What do you like when you hear a song? The way it makes you feel. Either sad, nostalgic, or energetic, you love a song because you felt something listening to it.

The sensation was basically free. You felt but it did not cost you. In the rest of life, whatever you felt is in reaction to a stimulus. There are choices, actions, and consequences. Reacting to a song, that was free hormones!

All musicians will tell you that music is built on specific structures and building blocks. For the note, the building blocks are called **chords**. For the rhythm and tempo, we have different musical **genres**. For how to play the note, we have **arpeggio**. If you mastered these, you can basically play all the music libraries of the world.

For those composing music and song, there are not inventing new music, the novelty is in the remixing of the chords, the arpeggio, and the rhythm to express a specific emotion. And you know what? Emotions, to be transferred successfully, have to be pure.

In other words, no one can sing a lie. They might be living a lie and crying their wounds in a song, but the emotions were real. Now you just have a way to filter the truth from the lies, at least at an individual level.

So no emotions are new and all of the chords have all been utilized in the past. Understand that to see the patterns and to read people and events. If you understand the construct of music, it is a great insight into our understanding of the **fabric of the Universe**.

Why? Because it is working. Music is a language, a frequency that moves us throughout time and space. It is one of the primal frequencies of the Universe. It is not the only frequency but one we can use to further push our understanding of Energy and the Universe.

0031
FROM SELFMADE
"Good things start to happen
when you say yes!"
Dr. Bak Nguyen

Even if I wrote this one in **SELFMADE**, my 35th book. I understood that one as I decided to reset myself, training, my education, and core values, saying **YES** to everything of 18 months. It was a way for me to do things differently and to get rid, once and for all, of my sorting system and gates.

You can find my entire story from week to week in the series **THE POWER OF YES**. I will not say that everything I did and everyone I met were good. They were possibilities and alternatives. Because I stayed open, now I know. I had a chance to feel and to understand.

To survive and be genuine to such a challenge saying **YES** to everything, I had to stop judging. Well, as I stopped judging others, I also cease judging myself. And that was the most powerful therapy one can experience.

Growth always happens at the giving end. Saying **YES**, I kept giving, my time, attention, affection, sometimes, even money. I was open, not dumb.

I must say that some of the most powerful people I know today started with saying **YES** to someone that I would not normally be open to. Even if what I thought of that person (the non-worthy one) concluded to be exact, being open allowed me to meet with more people, some of those I would have never meet otherwise. And that story happens more than once!

So yes, from my experience, good things start with a **YES** on your part. Now, be confident enough to open up and to keep your eyes open too! Being open does not mean to trust and believe everything people tell you, it just meant to be ready to listen and see first!

FAMOUS QUOTE 4

0061
FROM AFTERMATH
"In times of crisis, one has
to reinvent oneself."
Dr. Bak Nguyen

I found that one in the midst of COVID, isolated and confined home as the entire world came to a standstill for 3 months. Well, as I went online and connected with different leaders open to share and to seek solutions (they will eventually become **THE ALPHAS**), I noticed how easy it was to reach powerful and important people.

People that a few weeks ago were impossible to reach, well, within that unreal moment, were all available and seeking answers. By chance, I started connecting people and the interests (needs) of the moment and we built a network of brain and willpower linking the continents, the different industries, and even the different causes.

For as long as people were willing to share in the profit of a better world, **THE ALPHAS** were open to host and to empower. We were all united against an invisible enemy, COVID. For the first time in my lifetime, all interests were aligned.

I was a dentist, CEO, and world record author. Then COVID hit and I was stuck home with nothing but time and my internet connection. I went online and connected. In a matter of weeks, I reinvented myself into a host and an anchor of **THE ALPHAS**.

I met and interviewed so many powerful and smart people. In a matter of days, my reputation became international and my influence grew exponentially.

I was even elected one of the **top 100 doctors** of 2021. Well, usually all of this will not come together as fast but we were all in crisis and in pain. We welcomed change and we were seeking solutions. This is how I reinvented myself as a host, looking to change the world, this time, it was about helping the world to come back on its feet.

15 months after my first appearance as an **ALPHA**, there are talks between my team and Hollywood to bring the **ALPHASHOW** to **NETFLIX**, **Amazon Prime**, and the **big American Networks**. It is not done yet but it is a real possibility on the table.

15 months ago, I did not even know what a zoom call was. This is the power of saying **YES**, of acting **NOW**, and of being **flexible** to reinvent who we are, all combined into one single narrative.

Welcome to the Alphas.

0059
FROM SUCCESS IS A CHOICE
"Be bold, be flexible, act fast,
and stay humble."
Dr. Bak Nguyen

I am a believer that we can make our own destiny and chance. Nobody can ever say that I am an opportunist because most of the waves I surfed, I created myself. I did not create the problem, I created the solution, linking the dots in creative ways.

On that, I trust my instincts for the vision. I will say it out loud to listen to my own words and see if they make sense. That's why I need to be precise and bold. There is no space for doubt, nuances, and exceptions, not at that stage. Once the problem is clearly identified, the solution must be simple and easy to express. If not, it is not the right solution yet. That's step one.

Then, as I found an idea that survives the logical process of being express shortly and boldly, it is now about finding the quickest way to implement. Not the best way but the quickest way.

Keep in mind that we are still in experimental and prototype mode, we need to test and to readjust. What we don't know, we don't know, until we try. The sooner the better, because then, we will have **real data**. This is about being flexible. We might know the direction, we still have to figure out how to get there!

"I don't care if I am right, for as long as one of us is."
Dr. Bak Nguyen

And that is the kind of leadership and flexibility that I embody. To me, it is not about being right but about winning, about the outcome. Always as quickly as possible because until we reach a checkpoint, we are running on thin and borrowed resources.

And that's the humility part of that phrase, to understand that we are running on borrowed time and resources. The arrogance here will not only be to think that only we, have all the answers but also to stall looking for perfection… based on opinions.

Boldness and speed will protect you from the opinion part. Humility and flexibility will buy you the time your need to patch a solution together.

FAMOUS QUOTE 6

0067
FROM TORNADO
"History will say that to celebrate one world record,
we scored two more!"
Dr. Bak Nguyen

This is the Love story of William and I. Actually, this is a **Cinderella story for a father.** That year, I was celebrating a new world record, writing **15 books within 15 months**. I was exhausted and emptied. Then William asked me when are we writing our book together?

To keep my word to my son of 8, I was open and flexible to write **THE LEGEND OF THE CHICKEN HEART** together. I had no idea of how to write a story for children nor how to write with an 8-year-old.

Well because I was open and genuinely gave all of myself to the journey, we wrote the first 2 books of the chicken trilogy within a week. William was talking to SIRI (Apple) and I was listening to put into sentences the words of an 8-year-old telling the story of how can a chicken heart open its mind to become a lion heart.

I was moved to my core and was transported with the magic and the innocence of William, it replenished all of my energy. Within a week, we did more than write the books, I found a way to have the illustrations done too! It was the beginning of December and all the artists we just looking forward to the holiday break.

Well, they forced my hand and I had to take control. I bought royalty-free images and combined them in order to tell the story of the **CHICKEN HEART**, then the **LION HEART**, and the **DRAGON HEART**. Were had our trilogy done after 2 weeks of writing.

I could already see the ***world records*** coming in, not just for me but for William! His first trilogy was written in 2 weeks, at 8 years old. Then, Tranie, his mom, told me the sad news: William is failing his French classes with 55%!

I was perplexed. Between the world records and failing in French, I had a huge communication and branding problem on my hands. Not to forget his grades at school. What could I do?

Well, I had William translate all of the chicken books from English to French, one sentence after the next. By December 23 we were done: 2 trilogies, 1 in French and 1 in English telling the legends of the **CHICKEN HEART**, the **LION HEART**, and the **DRAGON HEART**.

And then, you won't believe what William asked me: he wanted more! I couldn't believe my ears! By chance, I bought many royalty-free images so I still have many that I haven't use yet. I went through the images and found enough to tell a 4th story: **WE ARE ALL DRAGONS**.

To William that is the story of the *ripple effect*. The chicken heart has become a lion heart. The lion heart has become a dragon heart. Now, the rest of the animals want to join and to become dragons too! He loved the idea.

To me, I always wanted to write a reboot of the TALES of LAFONTAINE. This was my chance. I made the imagery and showed them to my wife. I was bragging and expecting to be welcomed as a hero. I was so wrong.

Tranie flipped! She did not say a word until then but Christmas was coming and we had a trip planned for New York and to celebrate New Year on a cruise to the Bahamas. She did not want us to stress and spoil these much-needed family vacations on a fourth book.

William and I had to hide to write in secret. We celebrated Christmas, drove to New York City, spent a day shooting videos for the communcation of the **CHICKEN Trilogy** throughout New York, and embarked on the cruise. You can still see the videos online on my website (DrBakNguyen.com) or on William's Instagram profile.

We participated in each of the family activities and wrote in our spare time. Well, on the 31st, William and I, we isolated ourselves for the morning after breakfast and completed the French translation of the last book.

It was mission accomplished, we had written 8 children's books in 2 different languages within a month as co-authors, as father and son. After the completion, I asked William why he wanted to write more books. He said that he did not want our special connection to end. And he loved the fact that we had to hide from mama to write. It made us into real partners.

For my part, I told him why I accepted to push as far. We just completed the dragon's book and the dragon number is 8. In Asian culture, 8 is not only the **number of the dragon** but it is the infinite. Well, I am the father of the year giving to my son of 8, the infinite of wisdom and wealth for his first world records:

- Youngest author to write 8 children's books in 31 days
- Youngest author to write books in 2 different languages, French and English

And those were to celebrate my last world record writing **15 books in 15 months**, less than a month ago! That evening we had much to celebrate as people were joining for the countdown!

FAMOUS QUOTE 7

0069

FROM TORNADO

"Dream and the means will come."

Dr. Bak Nguyen

I wrote that one last year as I was running to complete my landmark world record of writing **72 books within 36 months**. **TORNADO** is all about momentum.

It will take another year, as William interviewed me for the writing of **TIMING, TIME MANAGEMENT ON STEROIDS** utilizing the **APOLLO protocol** before I clearly discover the secret of that quote.

To engage with William's interests, I needed to use examples that appeal to his imagination. He is 11 now, the chickens won't cut it anymore. So I use the metaphor of video games to explain that quote.

In racing games, we have a time to complete a part of the race and we need to cross the **checkpoints** before we run out of time. As we pass the **checkpoint**, more time is added to our timer and we can still keep going.

Well, in real life, it is exactly the same principle. We need to run on our resources until we cross a **checkpoint**. Then we will have more resources to keep going. The difference is that in real life, we need to establish our own **mapping** and **checkpoints**.

Let use the chicken book story as an example to illustrate the truth of this quote. We started writing 2 books together surfing on novelty and synergy. Then, we hit a road bump, no artist could deliver the needed imagery at our pace.

I had to dive into my resources and creativity to solve that void, which I did. I cross a **checkpoint** with my newfound solutions. It inspired both of us to finish all three books within 2 weeks, with the images.

Then, we hit another road bump as we learnt about William's failure in French. Because I was at a new *checkpoint* (world record for William), I have to address that problem quickly. This was not a father address the grades of his kid but a CEO addressing the branding and communication problem standing between him and his next win.

So I got William to translate all of his books in French. Since I was controlling the image and the text editing, and that we were both pumped from our recent wins, we made those within the next week, translating 3 children's books in French. Without the boost of energy of the new *checkpoint*, never we would have the motivation to do as much.

So now, we had 6 books written in 2 languages within 23 days! A new and even higher *checkpoint* was crossed. Then, William asked for more! He did not want to break our special connection and I was aiming for the **number of the dragon** as a special Christmas gift for William. We leveraged what we had as a boost in energy and went on for an extra round.

I had the images, we found a story and we did. Even the challenge that his mom was against the idea boosted our morale even more. We fuelled from that one too! We wrote History as father and son, as co-authors, as partners.

In this story, we jumped from win to win and we even leverage our liabilities to score as big!

FAMOUS QUOTE 8

0028
FROM THE BOOK OF LEGENDS, VOLUME 1
"We are all born little, as a chicken heart.
If we keep an open mind, we will grow into a lion heart. Some will choose to be close-minded and will remain small."
Dr. Bak Nguyen

Well, I decided to finish with this one since it was the core and the spin of the writing of the **CHICKENS BOOKS**, all 22 of them. We all know that the **CHICKENS BOOKS** elevated both William and me into legends. This is not bragging but a fact.

I needed a way to prove to you the **power of quotes**. Well, I can't think of a better one. A three theme phrases were the seeds with which I thought William his first philosophy lessons. Those he will never forget because he thinks that he was the one creating them!

He was 8 and it was Christmas time, with its exams and distractions. And yet, William's best gift that year was to spend time with his papa writing books. His words, not mine!

From a quote and mindset, we believed and walked the talk. 22 books and many world records scored on the way as we were pushing the boundaries, just because it was fun.

This changed William's present and future. He then spoke in front of a crowd of 300+ people to share his journey. He is legacy, not from receiving fortune at the death of a relative but from copying his dad.

To open his mind to grow from a chicken heart into a lion heart. Well, for the last 3 years, William is looking to act accordingly as a lion heart. Sure, I am helping from time to time but I am helping, he is the one at the wheel, of his own free will!

The effect was not just on him. That momentum allowed me to boost my numbers from 15 to 36 books, well I never slowed down. If today I can aspire to set the next world record of 100 books written within 4 years, I am still surfing from that win that I shared with William.

These 3 phrases combined as a quote changed both William's life and mine. Not to mention that it surely save my marriage… but this is a story for another book.

This is **Shortcut volume 7, Happiness**. Welcome to the Alphas.

Smile, that's the C major chord of the ballade.

Dr. BAK NGUYEN

PART 10

"FAMOUS QUOTES"

by Dr. BAK NGUYEN

0001

"The pain of the problem has to be greater than the pain of change."

Dr. Bak Nguyen

0002

"Sharing is the way to grow."

Dr. Bak Nguyen

0003

"One's legend can only begin the day one's Quest of Identity is over."

Dr. Bak Nguyen

0004

"Gratitude is the only past with a future."

Dr. Bak Nguyen

0005

"Mine was, forgive yourself."

Dr. Bak Nguyen

0006
"To walk on thin ice is a dangerous game.
To run is safer. To surf is the easiest."
Dr. Bak Nguyen

0007
"If I have changed the world from a dental chair,
you are all in a better position than I am
to change the world."
Dr. Bak Nguyen

0008
"The day you are fighting to raise the average instead
of beating it, that day, you've joined the leadership."
Dr. Bak Nguyen

0009
"At the end of the day, business is communication."
Dr. Bak Nguyen

0010
FROM INDUSTRIES' DISRUPTORS
"Make leverage of each of your liabilities,
and you will always be moving forward."
Dr. Bak Nguyen

0011
FROM INDUSTRIES' DISRUPTORS
"I believe in myself and I do it for God,
not the other way around."
Dr. Bak Nguyen

0012
FROM INDUSTRIES' DISRUPTORS
"Always choose the path of least resistance."
Dr. Bak Nguyen

0013
FROM INDUSTRIES' DISRUPTORS
"Be mindful of the consequences."
Dr. Bak Nguyen

0014
FROM CHANGING THE WORLD FROM A DENTAL CHAIR
"Hammering air three times over and
it will become steel."
Dr. Bak Nguyen

0015

"Mdex, for joy for life."

Dr. Bak Nguyen

0016

"Confidence is sexy."

Dr. Bak Nguyen

0017

"Make it happen!"

Dr. Bak Nguyen

0018

FROM THE POWER BEHIND THE ALPHA

"Humility is to know what you are and to recognize what you are not."

Dr. Bak Nguyen

0019

FROM MOMENTUM TRANSFER

"On thin ice, speed up, that's how you will eventually learn to fly! "

Dr. Bak Nguyen

0020

FROM MOMENTUM TRANSFER

"Control with wisdom is called influence."

Dr. Bak Nguyen

0021

FROM MOMENTUM TRANSFER

"To stabilize a momentum, speed up!"

Dr. Bak Nguyen

0022

FROM HYBRID

"Chords and patterns are the themes of the Universe."

Dr. Bak Nguyen

0023

FROM HYBRID

"A weakness is a strength out of reach."

Dr. Bak Nguyen

0024

FROM HYBRID

"Look for your next immediate win."

Dr. Bak Nguyen

0025
FROM REBOOT, TO GROW FROM MIDLIFE CRISIS

"Don't stop the flow of a river unless you are ready to clean up the flood."

Dr. Bak Nguyen

0026
FROM LEVERAGE COMMUNICATION INTO SUCCESS

"Find your worth in the service of others."

Dr. Bak Nguyen

0027
FROM LEVERAGE COMMUNICATION INTO SUCCESS

"Humility is not the denial of oneself but the acceptance of one true nature."

Dr. Bak Nguyen

0028
FROM THE BOOK OF LEGENDS, VOLUME 1

"We are all born little, as a chicken heart. If we keep an open mind, we will grow into a lion heart. Some will choose to be close-minded and will remain small."

Dr. Bak Nguyen

0029

FROM THE BOOK OF LEGENDS, VOLUME 1

"To have an open mind is step one.
To keep growing, one needs an open heart."

Dr. Bak Nguyen

0030

FROM THE BOOK OF LEGENDS, VOLUME 1

"Humility is the ability to recognize and to respect
what we are, and stop pretending to be
what we are not."

Dr. Bak Nguyen

0031

FROM SELFMADE

"Good things start to happen when you say yes!"

Dr. Bak Nguyen

0032

FROM SELFMADE

"Knowledge is the ground of the past.
Hope and Dreams are the air of the future."

Dr. Bak Nguyen

0033

FROM SELFMADE

"My deepest fear is to show up before God
and not have enough to show for."

Dr. Bak Nguyen

0034

FROM THE RISE OF THE UNICORN

"To make the world a better place."

Dr. Bak Nguyen

0035

FROM THE RISE OF THE UNICORN

"A Momentum is when it is easier
to keep moving than to stop."

Dr. Bak Nguyen

0036

FROM CHAMPION MINDSET

"I was open, and I bet on myself."

Dr. Bak Nguyen

0037

FROM HOW TO WRITE A BOOK IN 30 DAYS

"To keep Momentum, aim for the next win,
as little as it might be."

Dr. Bak Nguyen

0038

FROM HOW TO WRITE A BOOK IN 30 DAYS

"A quote is a truth from another life,
from a past legacy."

Dr. Bak Nguyen

0039

"The fewer the words, the better."

Dr. Bak Nguyen

0040

FROM POWER, EMOTIONAL INTELLIGENCE

"Align your emotions and your ambitions to be whole, to be unstoppable."

Dr. Bak Nguyen

0041

FROM POWER, EMOTIONAL INTELLIGENCE

"I believe in myself, and I do it for God, not the other way around."

Dr. Bak Nguyen

0042

FROM BRANDING

"I kept the "Dr." on to remind me to always put your interests before mine."

Dr. Bak Nguyen

0043

FROM BRANDING

"Arrogance is not the bragging of our knowledge, but rather the denial of our ignorance."

Dr. Bak Nguyen

0044

FROM HORIZON VOLUME ONE

"I treat people, not teeth."

Dr. Bak Nguyen

0045

FROM THE POWER OF YES, VOLUME 1

"Writing books allowed me to evolve
at the speed of my thoughts."

Dr. Bak Nguyen

0046

FROM THE POWER OF YES, VOLUME 1

"Speed is my power. Momentum, my expression."

Dr. Bak Nguyen

0047

FROM THE POWER OF YES VOLUME 3

"We do not need to choose, only to prioritize."

Dr. Bak Nguyen

0048

FROM HOW TO NOT FAIL AS A DENTIST

"Changing the world from a dental chair."

Dr. Bak Nguyen

0049
FROM HOW TO NOT FAIL AS A DENTIST
"I am not giving up, I am simply wising up!"

Dr. Bak Nguyen

0050
FROM HOW TO NOT FAIL AS A DENTIST
"With your money, do not trust anyone but yourself."

Dr. Bak Nguyen

0051
FROM HUMILITY FOR SUCCESS
"Reading will be cool again!"

Dr. Bak Nguyen

0052
FROM HUMILITY FOR SUCCESS
"Until it is done, it is air, good air but only air."

Dr. Bak Nguyen

0053
FROM MASTERMIND
"You can cheat, legally, by learning about shortcuts and leveraging."

Dr. Bak Nguyen

0054

FROM PLAYBOOK INTRODUCTION VOLUME 1

"Nothing will last forever, and nothing is free."

Dr. Bak Nguyen

0055

FROM PLAYBOOK INTRODUCTION VOLUME 2

"Be careful since doubts is a pet
that you are feeding."

Dr. Bak Nguyen

0056

FROM PLAYBOOK INTRODUCTION VOLUME 2

"Reach for your next win as soon as possible,
and build on it!"

Dr. Bak Nguyen

0057

FROM AMONGST THE ALPHAS, VOLUME 2

"Be bold, confident, and humble."

Dr. Bak Nguyen

0058

FROM AMONGST THE ALPHAS, VOLUME 2

"Growth happens at the giving end,
not the receiving one."

Dr. Bak Nguyen

0059

FROM SUCCESS IS A CHOICE

"Be bold, be flexible, act fast and stay humble."

Dr. Bak Nguyen

0060

FROM SUCCESS IS A CHOICE

"To succeed, be flexible."

Dr. Bak Nguyen

0061

FROM 90 DAYS CHALLENGE

"In times of crisis, one has to reinvent oneself."

Dr. Bak Nguyen

0062

FROM RISING

"To matter, serve."

Dr. Bak Nguyen

0063

FROM RISING

"There is no free money."

Dr. Bak Nguyen

0064

FROM AFTERMATH

"For the first time of our lifetime,
all the interests of the world are aligned."

Dr. Bak Nguyen

0065

FROM AFTERMATH

"In times of crisis, it is the perfect opportunity
to reinvent who we are. "

Dr. Bak Nguyen

0066

FROM AFTERMATH

"Yes, we can have it all!"

Dr. Bak Nguyen

0067

FROM TORNADO

"History will say that to celebrate one world record,
we scored two more!"

Dr. Bak Nguyen

0068

FROM TORNADO

"The only way to keep overdelivering
is playing, all-in!"

Dr. Bak Nguyen

0069

FROM TORNADO

"Dream and the means will come."

Dr. Bak Nguyen

0070

FROM ALPHA LADDERS VOLUME ONE

"All good things start with a YES."

Dr. Bak Nguyen

0071

FROM ALPHA LADDERS VOLUME 2

"Growth occurs at the giving end, always."

Dr. Bak Nguyen

0072

FROM THE CONFESSION OF AN OVERACHIEVER

"Being lazy doesn't mean that you don't have to do shit, it means that you don't have to go through shit to get things done."

Dr. Bak Nguyen

0073

FROM TO OVERACHIEVE EVERYTHING BEING LAZY

"Arrogance is not the recognition of who we are but the denial of what we are not."

Dr. Bak Nguyen

0074
FROM TO OVERACHIEVE EVERYTHING BEING LAZY
"You call me doctor to remind me to always put your needs before mine."
Dr. Bak Nguyen

0075
FROM TO OVERACHIEVE EVERYTHING BEING LAZY
"Nowadays, influence is power without liability."
Dr. Bak Nguyen

0076
FROM TO OVERACHIEVE EVERYTHING BEING LAZY
"I told you that everything in life is a trade. Be careful of what you are trading."
Dr. Bak Nguyen

0077
FROM SHORTCUT VOLUME 1 - HEALING
"Fear is a disease and it must be treated like one."
Dr. Bak Nguyen

This is **Shortcut volume 7, Happiness**. Welcome to the Alphas.

Smile, that's the C major chord of the ballade.

Dr. BAK NGUYEN

CONCLUSION

by Dr. BAK NGUYEN

This was by far the easiest of all the **SHORTCUT volumes** to write. I finished this one in about 24 hours, which will also set a new personal and world record. The first thing that I am asking myself is why? The previous volume, **POWER**, was so hard to complete, because of the laws of **TIMING** and the logic of **MAPPING**.

I started this journey saying that you have graduated, after the dark volume on **POWER**, you were ready to face anything. So was I.

Writing about happiness, we covered the themes of **HAPPINESS, LOVE, PARENTING**, and **TRAVELLING**. If those can be leveraged, aren't they powers too? The answer to that question is a little more complex than that.

First, we learnt that **HAPPINESS** is not a destination but a *birthright*, one we received with the gift of life. Seeking happiness, we blind ourselves to its existence looking at illusions and believing lies.

"Happiness is found and can only be felt in the present tense, neither it exists in the past nor the future."
Dr. Bak Nguyen

That's quote #2523. Looking at the past, people confuse happiness with nostalgia. Searching in the future, people confuse promise and happiness. Well, happiness is real and can be felt. Actually, because it is real and our body is producing hormones specific to that state of mind, there is our way to harness and leverage such power.

We are what we feel, remember? And since happiness is influenced by our perception of things and of Life, we can influence our own happiness by controlling our perception of life. That's the power and secret! That's the definition of a mindset.

Be happy first and you will feel powerful, not because you said it because your body produced the associate hormones. You can't lie or fool yourself into being happy.

What is sad is sad. You can either sit on that sadness for years until your life force fades away. You can also use that sad event as a way to combat procrastination and to jump into the unknown, looking for the answers you seek... why?!

And this is why this volume was so easy to write. **LOVE** is not a power, love is a powerful feeling that will push your body to produce hormones. That is the physical part of the love equation. On the logic side, **LOVE** is the best of **WHY**, of motivation to start and continue your walk, your journey.

The love I received from my parents and family built me up smart and strong. They gave me the best they could foresee. I accepted to be forged and molded, out of love and loyalty to them.

Then, I discovered true **Love** with a capital L. From that Love, I healed. On each occasion, I grew because I gave as much as I received.

Then, as I became a father, I grew even bigger and faster. Parenting is love, solely standing on the giving end. That's the mission, you love and give and hope for the best. As a father my love was not only a **WHY** but also a **HOW**. Because I was open to the idea of doing more, doing better, I grew. I did because my **WHY** was unconditional.

And **TRAVELLING**, well, I included travelling in the volume of **HAPPINESS** because it is one of the great way to quickly find happiness and to reset your entire being, mind, and body, to the present. You see, I told you that happiness only occurs in the present, because happiness is neither a souvenir nor a destination, happiness is a feeling! So is love and excitement.

Well, what is travelling but an excitement, an event to disrupt the settlements and the entitlements? **Happiness**, **Love**, **Parenting**, **Travelling** (excitement) are feelings to understand and to leverage from. But also, **TIMING** is so important too!

TIMING, that was the title of my 74th book. Well, the conclusion to **TIMING** is always **NOW**! Now as in the present tense. Your timing to rise and to take action is **now**. Your condition to be happy is to be available in the present moment. Past is souvenir and Future is projection, those will not generate the **hormones of happiness**!

This explain how writing this volume was so easy because I vibe in the present tense. Even if I retell events of the past, the emotions, the feeling, the comprehension were all about **now**, as I share with you.

And this is the ultimate power I am passing down to you, in three letters: **NOW**. Be available to feel and to be happy. Allow yourself to be happy, this is where your power will emerge. Other power can emerge from sadness, bitterness, and anger, but those will cost you many times over the power they will lend to you.

Remember that as much as power is lent, even rented, it is not something one can possess. On the contrary, it possesses you, as you are its vessel for a while. The feelings are yours to feel but you do not possess power, it possesses you! You can be power, you can't have power.

And this is reversed to the wording we used and are familiar with. The **corruption of power** started in our choice of wording. That was from the dark volume.

Now, from the light volume, **HAPPINESS**, happiness is a primal feeling, one we received as a birthright. Look for it and clean your excuses, denials, and lies. You know how to find your happiness. Let go of your anchor, shields, and filters. Feel the breeze and the warmth of the sun, there lays your happiness, in the present.

Your ballade awaits you. Smile and welcome the theme in C major! And a song is C major, well, it is usually a happy one!

This is **Shortcut volume 7, Happiness**. Welcome to the Alphas.

Smile, that's the C major chord of the ballade.

Dr. BAK NGUYEN

ANNEX

GLOSSARY OF Dr. BAK's LIBRARY

1

1SELF -080

REINVENT YOURSELF FROM ANY CRISIS
BY Dr. BAK NGUYEN

In 1SELF is about to reinvent yourself to rise from any crisis. Written in the midst of the COVID war, now more than ever, we need hope and the know-how to bridge the future. More than just the journey of Dr. Bak, this time, Dr. Bak is sharing his journey with mentors and people who built part of the world as we know it. Interviewed in this book, CHRISTIAN TRUDEAU, former CEO and FOUNDER of BCE EMERGIS (BELL CANADA), he also digitalized the Montreal Stock Exchange.RON KLEIN, American Innovator, inventor of the magnetic stripe of the credit card, of MLS (Multi-listing services) and the man who digitalized WALL STREET bonds markets.ANDRE CHATELAIN, former first vice-president of the MOVEMENT DES JARDINS. Dr. JEAN DE SERRES, former CEO of HEMA QUEBEC. These men created billions in values and have changed our lives, even without us knowing. They all come together to share their experiences and knowledge to empower each and everyone to emerge stronger from this crisis, from any crisis.

A

AFTERMATH -063
BUSINESS AFTER THE GREAT PAUSE
BY Dr. BAK NGUYEN & Dr. ERIC LACOSTE

In AFTERMATH, Dr. Bak joins forces with Community leader and philanthrope Dr. Eric Lacoste. Two powerful minds and forces of nature in the reaction to the worst economic meltdown in modern times. We are all victims of the CORONA virus. Both just like humans have learned to adapt to survive, so is our economy. Most business structures and management philosophies are inherited from the age of industrialization and beyond. COVID-19 has shot down the world economy with months. At the time of the AFTERMATH, the truth is many corporations and organizations will either have to upgrade to the INFORMATION AGE or disappear. More than the INFORMATION upgrade, the era of SOCIAL MEDIA and the MILLENNIALS are driving a revolution in the core philosophy of all organizations. Profit is not king anymore, support is. In this time and age where a teenager with a social account can compete with the million dollars PR firm, social implication is now the new cornerstone. Those who will adapt will prevail and prosper, while the resistance and old guards will soon be forgotten as fossils of a past era.

ALPHA LADDERS -075
CAPTAIN OF YOUR DESTINY
BY Dr. BAK NGUYEN & JONAS DIOP

In ALPHA LADDERS, Dr. Bak is sharing his private conversation and board meetings with 2 of his trusted lieutenants, strategist Jonas Diop and international Counsellor, Brenda Garcia. As both the Dr. Bak and ALPHA brands are gaining in popularity and traction, it was time to get the movement to the next level. Now, it's about building a community and to help everyone willing to become ALPHAS to find their powers. Dr. Bak is a natural recruiter of ALPHAS and peers. He also spent the last 20 years plus, training and mentoring proteges. Now comes the time to empower more and more proteges to become ALPHAS. ALPHAS LADDERS is the journey of how Dr. Bak went from a product of Conformity to rise into a force of Nature, know as a kind tornado. In ALPHA LADDERS Jonas pushed Dr. Bak to retrace each of the steps of his awakening, steps that we can breakdown and reproduce for ourselves. The goal is to empower each willing individual to become the ultimate Captain of his or her destiny, and to do it, again and again. Welcome to the Alphas.

ALPHA LADDERS 2 -081
SHAPING LEADERS AND ACHIEVERS
BY Dr. BAK NGUYEN & BRENDA GARCIA

In ALPHA LADDERS 2, Dr. Bak is sharing the second part of his private conversation and board meetings with his trusted lieutenants. This time it is with international Counsellor, Brenda Garcia that the dialogue is taking place. In this second tome, the journey is taken to the next level. If the first tome was about the WHYs and the HOWs at an individual level, this tome is about the WHYs and the HOWs at the societal level. Through the lens of her background in international relations and diplomacy, Brenda now has the mission to help Dr. Bak establish structures, not only for his emerging organization and legacy, THE ALPHAS, but to also inspire all the other leaders and structures of our society. To do this, Brenda is taking Dr. Bak on an anthropological, sociological and philosophical journey to revisit different historical key moments in various fields and eras, going as far back as in ancient Greece at the dawn of democracy, all the way to the golden era of modern multilateralism embodied by the UN structure. Learning from the legacies of prominent figures going from Plato to Ban Ki Moon, Martin Luther King or Nelson Mandela, to Machiavelli, Marx and Simone de Beauvoir, Brenda and Dr. Bak are attempting to grasp the essence of structure and hierarchy, their goal being to empower each willing individual to become the ultimate Captain of their own success, to climb up the ladders no matter how high it is, and to build their legacy one step at a time.

AMONGST THE ALPHAS -058
BY Dr. BAK NGUYEN, with Dr. MARIA KUNDSTATER, Dr. PAUL OUELLETTE and Dr. JEREMY KRELL

In AMONGST THE ALPHAS Dr. Bak opens the blueprint of the next level with the hope that everyone can be better, bigger, wiser, but above all, a philosophy of Life that if, well applied, can bring inspiration to life. The Alphas rose in the midst of the COVID war as an International Collaboration to empower individuals to rise from the global crisis. Joining Dr. Bak are some of the world thinkers and achievers, the Alphas. Doctors, business people, thinkers, achievers, influencers, they are coming together to define what is an Alpha and his or her role, making the world a better place. This isn't the American dream, it is the human dream, one that can help you make History. Joining Dr. Bak are 3 Alpha authors, Dr. Maria Kundstater, Dr. Paul Ouellette and Dr. Jeremy Krell. This book started with questions from coach Jonas Diop. Welcome to the Alphas.

AMONGST THE ALPHAS vol.2 -059
ON THE OTHER SIDE
BY Dr. BAK NGUYEN with Dr. JULIO REYNAFARJE, Dr. LINA DUSEVICIUTE and Dr. DUC-MINH LAM-DO

In AMONGST THE ALPHAS 2, Dr. Bak continues to explore the meaning of what it is to be an Alpha and how to act amongst Alphas, because as the saying taught us: alone one goes fast, together we goes far. Some people see the problem. Some people look at the problem, some people created the problem. Some people leverage the problem into solutions and opportunities. Well, all of those people are Alphas. Networking and leveraging one another, their powers and reach are beyond measure. And one will keep the other in line too. Joining Dr. Bak are 3 Alphas from around the world coming together to share and collaborate, Dr. DUSEVICIUTE, Dr. LAM-DO and Dr. REYNAFARJE. This isn't the American dream, it is the human dream, one that can help you make History. Welcome to the Alphas.

B

BOOTCAMP -071
BOOKS TO REWRITE MINDSETS INTO WINNING STATES OF MIND
BY Dr. BAK NGUYEN

In BOOTCAMP 8 BOOKS TO REWRITE MINDSETS INTO WINNING STATES OF MIND, Dr. Bak is taking you into his past, before the visionary entrepreneur, before the world records, before the Industry's disruptor status. Here are 8 of the books that changed Dr. Bak's thinking and, therefore, reset his evolution into the course we now know him for. BOOTCAMP: 8 BOOKS TO REWRITE MINDSETS INTO WINNING STATES OF MIND, is a Bootcamp of 8 weeks for anyone looking to experience Dr. Bak's training to become THE Dr. BAK you came to know and love. This book will summarize how each title changed Dr. Bak mindset into a state of mind and how he applied that to rewrite his destiny. 8 books to read, that's 8 weeks of Bootcamp to access the power of your MIND and of your WILL. Are you ready for a change?

BRANDING -044
BALANCING STRATEGY AND EMOTIONS
BY Dr. BAK NGUYEN

BRANDING is communication to its most powerful state. Branding is not just about communicating anymore but about making a promise, about establishing a relation, about generating an emotion. More than once, Dr. Bak proved himself to be a master, communicating and branding his ideas into flags attracting interest and influences, nationally and internationally. In BRANDING, Dr. Bak shares a very unique and personal journey, branding Dr. Bak. How does he go from Dr. Nguyen, a loved and respected dentist to becoming Dr. Bak, a world anchor hosting THE ALPHAS in the medical and financial world? More than a personal journey, BRANDING helps to break down the steps to elevate someone with nothing else but the force of his or her spirit. Welcome to the Alphas.

C

CHANGING THE WORLD FROM A DENTAL CHAIR -007
BY Dr. BAK NGUYEN

Since he has received the EY's nomination for entrepreneur of the year for his startup Mdex & Co, Dr. Bak Nguyen has pushed the opportunity to the next level. Speaker, author, and businessman, Dr. Bak is a true entrepreneur and industries' disruptor. To compensate for the startup's status of Mdex & Co, he challenged himself to write a book based on the EY's questionnaire to share an in-depth vision of his company. With "Changing the World from a dental chair" Dr. Bak is sharing his thought process and philosophy to his approach to the industry. Not looking to revolutionize but rather to empower, he became, despite himself, an industries disruptor: an entrepreneur who has established a new benchmark. Dr. Bak Nguyen is a cosmetic dentist and visionary businessman who won the GRAND HOMAGE prize of "LYS de la Diversité" 2016, for his contribution as a citizen and entrepreneur in the community. He also holds recognitions from the Canadian Parliament and the Canadian Senate.

In 2003, he founded Mdex, a dental company upon which in 2018, he launched the most ambitious private endeavour to reform the dental industry, Canada wide. He wrote seven books covering ENTREPRENEURSHIP, LEADERSHIP, QUEST of IDENTITY, and now, PROFESSION HEALTH. Philosopher, he has close to his heart the quest of happiness of the people surrounding him, patients, and colleagues alike. Those projects have allowed Dr. Nguyen to attract interests from the international and diplomatic community and he is now the centre of a global discussion on the wellbeing and the future of the health profession. It is in that matter that he shares with you his thoughts and encourages the health community to share their own stories.

CHAMPION MINDSET -039
LEARNING TO WIN
BY Dr. BAK NGUYEN & CHRISTOPHE MULUMBA

CHAMPION MINDSET is the encounter of the business world and the professional sports world. Industries' Disruptor Dr. BAK NGUYEN shares his wisdom and views with the HAMMER, CFL Football Star, Edmonton's Eskimos CHRISTOPHE MULUMBA on how to leverage on the champion mindset to create successful entrepreneurs. Writing and challenging each other, they discovered the parallels and the difference of both worlds, but mainly, the recipe for leveraging from one to succeed in the other, from champions and entrepreneurs to WINNERS. Build and score your millions, it is a matter of mindset! This is CHAMPION MINDSET.

E

EMPOWERMENT -069
BY Dr. BAK NGUYEN

In EMPOWERMENT, Dr. Bak's 69th book, writing a book every 8 days for 8 weeks in a row to write the next world record of writing 72 books/36 months, Dr. Bak is taking a rest, sharing his inner feelings, inspiration, and motivation. Much more than his dairy, EMPOWERMENT is the key to walk in his footsteps and to comprehend the process of an overachiever. Dr. Bak's helped and inspired countless people to find their voice, to live their dream, and to be the better version of themselves. Why is he sharing as much and keep sharing? Why is he going that fast, always further and further, why and how is he keeping his inspiration and momentum? Those are all the answers EMPOWERMENT will deliver to you. This book might be one of the fastest Dr. Bak has written, not because of time constraints but from inspiration, pure inspiration to share and to grow. There is always a dark side to each power, two faces to a coin. Well, this is the less prominent facets of Dr. Bak Momentum and success, the road to his MINDSET.

F

FORCES OF NATURE -015
FORGING THE CHARACTER OF WINNERS
BY Dr. BAK NGUYEN

In FORCES OF NATURE, Dr. Bak is giving his all. This is his 15 books written within 15 months. It is the end of a marathon to set the next world record. For the occasion, he wanted to end with a big bang! How about a book with all of his biggest challenges? A Quest of Identity, a journey looking for his name and powers, Dr. Bak is borrowing with myths and legends to make this journey universal. Yes, this is Dr. Bak's mythology. Demons, heroes and Gods, there are forces of Nature that we all meet on our way for our name. Some will scare us, some will fight us, some will manipulate us. We can flee, we can hide, we can fight. What we do will define our next encounter and the one after. A tale of personal growth, a journey to find power and purpose, Dr. Bak is showing us the path to freedom, the Path of Life. Welcome to the Alphas.

H

HORIZON, BUILDING UP THE VISION -045
VOLUME ONE
BY Dr. BAK NGUYEN

Dr. Bak is opening up at your demand! Many of you are following Dr. Bak online and are asking to know more about his lifestyle. This is how he has chosen to respond: sharing his lifestyle as he traveled the world and what he learned in each city to come to build his Mindset as a driver and a winner. Here are 10 destinations (over 69 that will be following in the next volumes...) in which he shares his journey. New York, Quebec, Paris, Punta Cana, Monaco, Los Angeles, Nice, Holguin, the journey happened over twenty years.

HORIZON, ON THE FOOTSTEP OF TITANS -048
VOLUME TWO
BY Dr. BAK NGUYEN

Dr. Bak is opening up at your demand! Many of you are following Dr. Bak online and are asking to know more about his lifestyle. This is how he has chosen to respond: sharing his lifestyle as he traveled the world and what he learned in each city to come to build his Mindset as a driver and a winner. Here are 9 destinations (over 72 that will be following in the next volumes...) in which he shares his journey. Hong Kong, London, Rome, San Francisco, Anaheim, and more..., the journey happened over twenty years. Dr. Bak is sharing with you his feelings, impressions, and how they shaped his state of mind and character into Dr. Bak. From a dreamer to a driver and a builder, the journey started since he was 3. Wealth is a state of mind, and a state of mind is the basis of the drive. Find out about the mind of an Industry's disruptor.

HORIZON, DREAMING OF THE FUTURE -068
VOLUME THREE
BY Dr. BAK NGUYEN

Dr. Bak is back. From the midst of confinement, he remembers and writes about what life was, when traveling was a natural part of Life. It will come back. Now more than ever, we need to open both our hearts and minds to fight fear and intolerance. Writing from a time of crisis, he is sharing the magic and psychological effect of seeing the world and how it has shaped his mindset. Here are 9 other destinations (over 75) in which he shares his journey. Beijing, Key West, Madrid, Amsterdam, Marrakech and more..., the journey happened over twenty years.

HOW TO NOT FAIL AS A DENTIST -047
BY Dr. BAK NGUYEN

In HOW TO NOT FAIL AS A DENTIST, Dr. Bak is given 20 plus years of experience and knowledge of what it is to be a dentist on the ground. PROFESSIONAL INTELLIGENCE, FINANCIAL INTELLIGENCE and MANAGEMENT INTELLIGENCE are the fields that any dentist will have to master for a chance to success and a shot for happiness practicing dentistry. Where ever you are starting your career as a new graduate or a veteran in the field looking to reach the next level, this is book smart and street smart all into one. This is Million Dollar Mindset applied to dentistry. We won't be making a millionaire out of you from this book, we will be giving you a shot to happiness and success. The million will follow soon enough.

HOW TO WRITE A BOOK IN 30 DAYS -042
BY Dr. BAK NGUYEN

In HOW TO WRITE YOUR BOOK IN 30 DAYS, Dr. Bak has crafted writing skills and techniques that can be shared and mastered. This book is mainly about structure and how to keep moving forward, avoiding the hit of the INSPIRATION WALL. You will find a wealth of wisdom from his experience writing your first, second, or even 10th book. Dr. Bak is sharing his secrets writing books, having written himself 72 books within 36 months. Visionary businessman, doctor in dentistry, Dr. Bak describes himself as a Dentist by circumstances, a communicator by passion, and an entrepreneur by nature.

HOW TO WRITE A SUCCESSFUL BUSINESS PLAN -049
BY Dr. BAK NGUYEN & ROUBA SAKR

In HOW TO WRITE A SUCCESSFUL BUSINESS PLAN, Dr. Bak is given 20 plus years of experience and knowledge of what it is to be an entrepreneur and more importantly, how to have the investors and banks on your side. Being an entrepreneur is surely not something you learn from school, but there are steps to master so you can communicate your views and vision. That's the only way you will have financing.Writing a business is only not a mandatory stop only for the bankers, but an essential step to every entrepreneur, to know the direction and what's coming next. A business plan is also not set in stone, if there is a truth in business is that nothing will go as planned. Writing down your business plan the first time will prepare you to adapt and to overcome the challenges and surprises. For most entrepreneurs, a business is a passion. To most investors and all banks, a business is a system. Your business plan is the map to that system. However unique your ideas and business are, the mapping follows the same steps and pattern.

HUMILITY FOR SUCCESS -051
BALANCING STRATEGY AND EMOTIONS
BY Dr. BAK NGUYEN

HUMILITY FOR SUCCESS is exploring the emotional discomforts and challenges champions, and overachievers put themselves through. Success is never done overnight and on the way, just like the pain and the struggles aren't enough, we are dealing with the doubts, the haters, and those who like to tell us how to live our lives and what to do. At the same time, nothing of worth can be achieved alone. Every legend has a cast of characters, allies, mentors, companions, rivals, and foes. So one needs the key to social behaviour. HUMILITY FOR SUCCESS is exploring the matter and will help you sort out beliefs from values, peers from friends. Humility is much more about how we see ourselves than how others see us. For any entrepreneur and champion, our daily is to set our mindset right, and to perfect our skills, not to fit in. There is a world where CONFIDENCE grows is in synergy with HUMILITY. As you set the right label on the right belief, you will be able to grow and to leave the lies and haters far behinds. This is HUMILITY FOR SUCCESS.

HYBRID -011
THE MODERN QUEST OF IDENTITY
BY Dr. BAK NGUYEN

IDENTITY -004
THE ANTHOLOGY OF QUESTS
BY Dr. BAK NGUYEN

What if John Lennon was still alive and running for president today? What kind of campaign will he be running? IDENTIFY -THE ANTHOLOGY OF QUESTS is about the quest each of us has to undertake, sooner or later, THE QUEST OF IDENTITY. Citizen of the world, aim to be one, the one, one whole, one unity, made of many. That's the anthology of life! Start with your one, find your unity, and your legend will start. We are all small-minded people anyway! We need each other to be one! We need each other to be happy, so we, so you, so I, can be happy. This is the chorus of life. This is our song! Citizens of the world, I salute you! This is the first tome of the IDENTITY QUEST. FORCES OF NATURE (tome 2) will be following in SUMMER 2021. Also under development, Tome 3 - THE CONQUEROR WITHIN will start production soon.

INDUSTRIES DISRUPTORS -006
BY Dr. BAK NGUYEN

INDUSTRIES DISRUPTORS is a strange title, one that sparkles mixed feelings. A disruptor is someone making a difference, and since we, in general, do not like change, the label is mostly negative. But a disruptor is mostly someone who sees the same problem and challenge from another angle. The disruptor will tackle that angle and come up with something new from something existent. That's evolution! In INDUSTRIES DISRUPTORS, Dr. Bak is joining forces with James Stephan-Usypchuk to share with us what is going on in the minds and shoes of those entrepreneurs disrupting the old habits. Dr. Bak is changing the world from a dental chair, disrupting the dental, and now the book industry. James is a maverick in the Intelligence space, from marketing to Artificial Intelligence. Coming from very different backgrounds and industries, they end up telling very similar stories. If disruptors change the world, well, their story proves that disruptors can be made and forged. Here's the recipe. Here are their stories.

K

KRYPTO -040
TO SAVE THE WORLD
BY Dr. BAK NGUYEN & ILYAS BAKOUCH

L

LEADERSHIP -003
PANDORA'S BOX
BY Dr. BAK NGUYEN

LEADERSHIP, PANDORA'S BOX is 21 presidential speeches for a better tomorrow for all of us. It aims to drive HOPE and motivation into each and every one of us. Together we can make the difference, we hold such power. Covering themes from LOYALTY to GENEROSITY, from FREEDOM and INTELLIGENCE to DOUBTS and DEATH, this is not the typical presidential or motivational speeches that we are used to. LEADERSHIP PANDORA'S BOX will surf your emotions first, only to dive with you to touch the core and soul of our meaning: to matter. This is not a Quest of Identity, but the cry to rally as a species, to raise our heads toward the future, and to move forward as a WHOLE. Not a typical Dr. Bak's book, LEADERSHIP, PANDORA'S BOX is a must-read for all of you looking for hope and purpose, all of us, citizens of the world.

LEVERAGE -014
COMMUNICATION INTO SUCCESS
BY Dr. BAK NGUYEN

In LEVERAGE COMMUNICATION TO SUCCESS, Dr. Bak shares his secret and mindsets to elevate an idea into a vision and a vision into an endeavour. Some endeavours will be a project, some others will become companies, and some will grow into a movement. It does not matter, each started with great communication.Communication is a very vast concept, education, sale, sharing, empowering, coaching, preaching, entertaining. Those are all different kinds of communication. The intent differs, the audiences vary, the messages are unique but the frame can be templated and mastered. In LEVERAGE COMMUNICATION TO SUCCESS, Dr. Bak is loyal to his core, sharing only what he knows best, what he has done himself. This book is dedicated to communicating successfully in business.

M

MASTERMIND, 7 WAYS INTO THE BIG LEAGUE -052
BY Dr. BAK NGUYEN & JONAS DIOP

MASTERMIND, 7 WAYS INTO THE BIG LEAGUE is the result of the encounter of business coach Jonas Diop and Dr. Bak. As a professional podcaster and someone always seeking the truth and ways to leverage success and performance, coach Jonas is putting Dr. Bak to the test, one that should reveal his secret to overachieve month after month, accumulating a new world record every month. Follow those two great minds as they push each other to surpass themselves, each in their own way and own style. MASTERMIND, 7 WAYS INTO THE BIG LEAGUE is more than a roadmap to success, it is a journey and a live testimony as you are turning the pages, one by one.

MIDAS TOUCH -065
POST-COVID DENTISTRY
BY Dr. BAK NGUYEN, Dr. JULIO REYNAFARJE AND Dr. PAUL OUELLETTE

MIDAS TOUCH, is the memoir of what happened in the ALPHAS SUMMIT in the midst of the GREAT PAUSE as great minds throughout the world in the dental field are coming together. As the time of competition is obsolete, the new era of collaboration is blooming. This is the 3rd book of the ALPHAS, after AFTERMATH and RELEVANCY, all written in the midst of confinement. Dr. Julio Reynafarje is bearing this initiative, to share with you the secret of a successful and lasting relationship with your patients, balancing science and psychology, kindness, and professionalism. He personally invited the ALPHAS to join as co-author, Dr. Paul Ouellette, and Dr.

Paul Dominique, and Dr. Bak.Together, they have more than 100 years of combined experience, wisdom, trade, skills, philosophy, and secrets to share with you to empower you in the rebuilding of the dental profession in the aftermath of COVID. RELEVANCY was about coming together and to rebuild the future. MIDAS TOUCH is about how to build, one treatment plan at a time, one story at a time, one smile at a time.

MINDSET ARMORY -050
BY Dr. BAK NGUYEN

MINDSET ARMORY is Dr. Bak's 49th book, days after he completed his world record of writing 48 books within 24 months, on top of being a CEO of Mdex & Co and a full-time cosmetic dentist. Dr. Bak is undoubtedly an OVERACHIEVER. From his last books, he has shared more and more of his lifestyle and how it forged his winning mindset. Within MINDSET ARMORY, Dr. Bak is sharing with us his tools, how he found them, forged them, and leverage them. Just like any warrior needs a shield, a sword, and a ride, here are Dr. Bak's. For any entrepreneur, the road to success is a long and winding journey. On the way, some will find allies and foes. Some allies will become foes, and some foes might become allies. In today's competitive world, the only constant is change. With the right tool, it is possible to achieve. The right tool, the right mindset. This is MINDSET ARMORY.

MIRROR -085
BY Dr. BAK NGUYEN

MIRROR is the theme for a personal book. Not only to Dr. Bak but to all of us looking to reach beyond who and what we actually are. MIRROR is special in the fact that it is not only the content of the book that is of worth but the process in which Dr. Bak shared his own evolution. To go beyond who we are, one must grow every day. And how do you compare your growth and how far have you reach? Looking in the mirror. In all of Dr. Bak's writing, looking at the past is a trap to avoid at all costs. Looking in the mirror, is that any better? Share Dr. Bak's way to push and keep pushing himself without friction nor resistance. Please read that again. To evolve without friction or resistance... that is the source of infinite growth and the unification of the Quest for Power and the Quest of Happiness.

MOMENTUM TRANSFER -009
BY Dr. BAK NGUYEN & Coach DINO MASSON

How to be successful in your business and in your life? Achieve Your Biggest Goals With MOMENTUM TRANSFER. START THE BUSINESS YOU WANT - AND BRING IT NEXT LEVEL! GET THE LIFE YOU ALWAYS WANTED - AND IMPROVE IT! TAKE ANY PROJECTS YOU HAVE - AND MAKE IT THE BEST! In this powerful book, you'll discover what a small business owner learned from a millionaire and successful entrepreneur. He applied his mentor's principles and is explaining them in full detail in this book. The small business owner wrote the book he has always wanted to read and went from the verge of bankruptcy to quadrupling his revenues in less than 9 months and improve his personal life by increasing his energy and bring back peacefulness. Together, the millionaire and the small business owner are sharing their most valuable business and life lessons to the world. The most powerful book to increase your momentum in your business and your life introduces simple and radical life-changing concepts: Multiply your business revenues by finding the Eye of your Momentum - Increase your energy by building and feeding your own Momentum - How to increase your confidence with these simple steps - How to transfer your new powerful energy into other aspects of your business and life - How to set goals and achieve them (even crush them!)- How to always tap into an effortless and limitless force within you- And much, much more!

P

PLAYBOOK INTRODUCTION -055
BY Dr. BAK NGUYEN

In PLAYBOOK INTRODUCTION, Dr. Bak is open the door to all the newcomers and aspirant entrepreneurs who are looking at where and when to start. Based on questions of two college students wanting to know how to start their entrepreneurial journey, Dr. Bak dives into his experiences to empower the next generation, not about what they should do, but how he, Dr. Bak, would have done it today. This is an important aspect to recognize in the business world, the world has changed since the INFORMATION AGE and the advent of the millenniums into the market. Most matrix and know-how have to be adapted to today's speed and accessibility to the information. We are living at the INFORMATION AGE, this book is the precursor to the ABUNDANCE AGE, at least to those open to embrace the opportunity.

PLAYBOOK INTRODUCTION 2 -056
BY Dr. BAK NGUYEN

In PLAYBOOK INTRODUCTION 2, Dr. Bak continuing the journey to welcome the newcomers and aspirant entrepreneurs looking at where and when to start. If the first volume covers the mindset, the second is covering much more in-depth the concept of debt and leverage.This is an important aspect to recognize in the business world, the world has changed since the INFORMATION AGE and the advent of the millenniums into the market. Most matrix and know-how have to be adapted to today's speed and accessibility to the information. We are living at the INFORMATION AGE, this book is the precursor to the ABUNDANCE AGE, at least to those open to embrace the opportunity.

POWER -043
EMOTIONAL INTELLIGENCE
BY Dr. BAK NGUYEN

IN POWER, EMOTIONAL INTELLIGENCE, Dr. Bak is sharing his experiences and secrets leveraging on his EMOTIONAL INTELLIGENCE, a power we all have within. From SYMPATHY, having others opening up to you, to ACTIVE LISTENING, saving you time and energy; from EMPATHY, allowing you to predict the future to INFLUENCE, enabling you to draft the future, not to forget the power of the crowd with MOMENTUM, you are now in possession of power in tune with nature, yourself. It is a unique take on the subject to empower you to find your powers and your destiny. Visionary businessman, doctor in dentistry, Dr. Bak describes himself as a Dentist by circumstances, a communicator by passion, and an entrepreneur by nature.

POWERPLAY -078
HOW TO BUILD THE PERFECT TEAM
BY Dr. BAK NGUYEN

In POWERPLAY, HOW TO BUILD THE PERFECT TEAM, Dr. Bak is sharing with you his experience, perspective, and mistake traveling the journey of the entrepreneur. A serial entrepreneur himself, he started venture only with a single partner as team to build companies with a director of human resources and a board of directors. POWERPLAY is not a story, it is the HOW TO build the perfect team, knowing that perfection is a lie. So how can one build a team that will empower his or her vision? How to recruit, how to train, how to retain? Those are all legitimate questions. And all of those won't matter if the first question isn't answered: what is the reason for the team? There is the old way to hire and the new way to recruit. Yes, Human Resources is all about mindset too! This journey is one of introspection, of leadership, and a cheat sheet to build, not only the perfect team but the team that will empower your legacy to the next level.

PROFESSION HEALTH - TOME ONE -005
THE UNCONVENTIONAL QUEST OF HAPPINESS
BY Dr. BAK NGUYEN, Dr. MIRJANA SINDOLIC, Dr. ROBERT DURAND AND COLLABORATORS

Why are health professionals burning out while they give the best of themselves to heal the world? Dr. Bak aims to break the curse of isolation that health professionals face and establish a conversation to start the healing process. PROFESSION HEALTH is the basis of an ongoing discussion and will also serve as an introduction to a study lead by Professor Robert Durand, DMD, MSc Science from University of Montreal, study co-financed by Mdex and the Federal Government of Canada. Co-writers are Dr. Mirjana Sindolic, Professor Robert Durand, Dr. Jean De Serres, MD and former President of Hema Quebec, Counsel-Minister Luis Maria Kalaff Sanchez, Dr. Miguel Angel Russo, MD, Banker Anthony Siggia, Banker Kyles Yves, and more...
This is the first Tome of three, dedicated to help "WHITE COATS" to heal and to find their happiness.

R

REBOOT -012
MIDLIFE CRISIS
BY Dr. BAK NGUYEN

MidLife Crisis is a common theme to each of us as we reach the threshold. As a man, as a woman, why is it that half of the marriages end up in recall? If anything else would have half those rates of failure, the lawsuits would be raining. Where are the flaws, the traps? Love is strong and pure, why is marriage not the reflection of that? All hard to ask questions with little or no answers. Dr. Bak is sharing his reflections and findings as he reached himself the WALL OF MARRIAGE. This is a matter that affects all of our lives. It is time for some answers.

RELEVANCY - TOME TWO -064
REINVENTING OURSELVES TO SURVIVE
BY Dr. BAK NGUYEN & Dr. PAUL OUELLETTE AND COLLABORATORS

THE GREAT PAUSE was a reboot of all the systems of society. Many outdated systems will not make it back. The Dental Industry is a needed one, it has laid on complacency for far too long. In an age where expertise is global and democratized and can be replaced with technologies and artificial intelligence, the REBOOT will force, not just an update, but an operating system replacement and a firmware upgrade.First, they saved their industry with THE ALPHAS INITIATIVE, sharing their knowledge and vision freely to all the world's dental industry. With the OUELLETTE INITIATIVE, they bought some time to all the dental clinics to resume and to adjust. The warning has been given, the clock is now ticking. who will prevail and prosper and who will be left behind, outdated and obsolete?

RISING -062
TO WIN MORE THAN YOU ARE AFRAID TO LOSE
BY Dr. BAK NGUYEN

In RISING, TO WIN MORE TAN YOU ARE AFRAID TO LOSE, Dr. Bak is breaking down the strategy to success to all, not only those wearing white coats and scrubs. More than his previous book (SUCCESS IS A CHOICE), this one is covering most of the aspects of getting to the next level, psychologically, socially, and financially. Rising is broken down into three key strategies: Financial Leverage - Compressing time - Always being in control. Presented by MILLION DOLLAR MINDSET, the book is covering more than the ways to create wealth, but also how to reach happiness and to live a life without regrets. Dr. Bak the CEO and founder of Mdex & Co, a company with the promise of reforming the whole dental industry for the better. He wrote more than 60 books within 30 months as he is sharing his experiences, secrets, and wisdom.

S

SELFMADE -036
GRATITUDE AND HUMILITY
BY Dr. BAK NGUYEN

This is the story of Dr. Bak, an artist who became a dentist, a dentist who became an Entrepreneur, an Entrepreneur who is seeking to save an entire industry.In his free time, Dr. Bak managed to write 37 books and is a contender to 3 world records to be confirmed. Businessman and visionary, his views and philosophy are ahead of our time. This is his 37th book. In SELFMADE, Dr. Bak is answering the questions most entrepreneurs want to know, the HOWTO and the secret recipes, not just to succeed, but to keep going no matter what! SELFMADE is the perfect read for any entrepreneurs, novices, and veterans.

SHORTCUT vol. 1 - HEALING -093
BY Dr. BAK NGUYEN

In SHORTCUT 408 HEALING QUOTES, Dr. Bak revisits and compiles his journey of healing and growing. Just anyone, he was molded and shaped by Conformity and Society to the point of blending and melting. Walking his journey of healing, he rediscovers himself and found his true calling. And once whole with himself and with the Universe, Dr. Bak found his powers. In SHORTCUT 408 HEALING QUOTES, you have a quick and easy way to surf his mindsets and what allowed him to heal, to find back his voice and wings, and to walk his destiny. You too are walking your Quest of Identity. That one is mainly a journey of healing. May you find yours and your powers.

SHORTCUT vol. 2 - GROWING -094
BY Dr. BAK NGUYEN

In SHORTCUT 408 GROWTH QUOTES, Dr. Bak is compiling his library of books about personal growth and self-improvement. More than a motivational book, more than a compilation of knowledge, Dr. Bak is sharing the mindsets upon which he found his power to achieve and to overachieve. We all have our powers, only they were muted and forgotten as we were forged by Conformity and Society. After the healing process, walking your Quest of Identity, the Quest for you growth and God given power is next to lead you to walk your Destiny.

SHORTCUT vol. 3 - LEADERSHIP -095
BY Dr. BAK NGUYEN

In SHORTCUT 365 LEADERSHIP QUOTES, Dr. Bak is compiling his library of books about leadership and ambition. Yes, the ambition is to find your worth and to make the world a better place for all of us. If the 3rd volume of SHORTCUT is mainly a motivational compilation, it also holds the secrets and mindsets to influence and leadership. If you were looking to walk your legend and to impact the world, you are walking a lonely path.

You might on your own, but it does not have to be harder than it is. As we all have your unique challenges, the key to victory is often found in the same place, your heart. And here are 365 shortcuts to keep you believing and to attract more people to you as you are growing into a true leader.

SHORTCUT vol. 4 - CONFIDENCE-096
BY Dr. BAK NGUYEN

SHORTCUT 518 CONFIDENCE QUOTES, is the most voluminous compilation of Dr. Bak's quotes. To heal was the first step. To grow and find your powers came next. As you are walking your personal legend, Confidence is both your sword and armour to conquer your Destiny and to overcome all of the challenges on your way. In SHORTCUT volume four, Dr. Bak comprises all his mindsets and wisdom to ease your ascension. Confidence is not something one is simply born with, but something to nurture, grow, and master. Some will have the chance to be raised by people empowering Confidence, others will have to heal from Conformity to grow their confidence. It does not matter, only once Confident, can one stand tall and see clearly the horizon.

SHORTCUT vol. 5- SUCCESS-097
BY Dr. BAK NGUYEN

Success is not a destination but a journey and a side effect. While no map can lead you to success, the right mindset will forge your own success, the one without medals nor labels. If you are looking to walk your legend, to be successful is merely the beginning. Actually, being successful is often a side effect of the mindsets and actions that you took, you provoked. In SHORTCUT 317 SUCCESS QUOTES, Dr. Bak is revisiting his journey, breaking down what led him to be successful despite the odds stacked against him. As success is the consequence of mindsets, choices, and actions, it can be duplicated over and over again, one just needs to master the mindsets first.

SHORTCUT vol. 6- POWER-098
BY Dr. BAK NGUYEN

That's the kind of power that you will discover within this journey. Power is a tool, a leverage. Well used, it will lead to great achievements. Misused, it will be your downfall. If a sword sometimes has 2 edges, Power is a sword with no handle and multiple edges. You have been warned. In SHORTCUT 376 POWER QUOTES, Dr. Bak is compiling all the powers he found and mastered walking his own legend. If the first power was Confidence, very quickly, Dr. Bak realized that Confidence was the key to many, many more powers. Where to find them, how to yield them, and how to leverage these powers is the essence of the 6th volume of SHORTCUT.

SHORTCUT vol. 7- HAPPINESS-099
BY Dr. BAK NGUYEN

We were all born happy and then, somehow, we lost our ways and forgot our ways home. Is this the real tragedy behind the lost paradise myth? If we were happy once, we can trust our heart to find our way home, once more. This is the journey of the 7th volume of the SHORTCUT series. In SHORTCUT 306 HAPPINESS QUOTES, Dr. Bak is revisiting and compiling all the secrets and mindsets leading to happiness. Happiness is not just a destination but a shrine for Confidence and a safe place to regroup, to heal, to grow. We each have our own happiness. What you will learn here is where to find yours and, more importantly, how to leverage you to ease the journey ahead, because happiness is not your final destination. It can be the key to your legend.

SHORTCUT vol. 8- DOCTORS-100
BY Dr. BAK NGUYEN

If healing was the first step to your destiny and powers, there is a science to heal. Those with that science are doctors, the healers of the world. In India, healers are second only to the Gods! In SHORTCUT 170 DOCTOR QUOTES, Dr. Bak is dedicating the 8th volume of the series to his peers, doctors, from all around the world. Doctors too, have to walk their Quest of Identity, to heal from their pain and to walk their legend. Doctors need to heal and rejuvenate to keep healing the world. If healing is their science, in SHORTCUT, they will access the power of leveraging.

SUCCESS IS A CHOICE -060
BLUEPRINTS FOR HEALTH PROFESSIONALS
BY Dr. BAK NGUYEN

In SUCCESS IS A CHOICE, FINANCIAL MILLIONAIRE BLUEPRINTS FOR HEALTH PROFESSIONALS, Dr. Bak is breaking down the strategy to success for all those wearing white coats and scrubs: doctors, dentists, pharmacists, chiropractors, nurses, etc. Success is broken down into three key strategies: Financial Leverage - Compressing time - Always being in control. Presented by MILLION DOLLAR MINDSET, the book is covering more than the ways to create wealth, but also how to reach happiness and to live a life without regrets.Dr. Bak is a successful cosmetic dentist with nearly 20 years of experience. He founded Mdex & Co, a company with the promise of reforming the whole dental industry for the better. While doing so, he discovered a passion for writing and for sharing. Multiple times World Record, Dr. Bak is writing a book every 2 weeks for the last 30 months. This is his 60th book, and he is still practicing. How he does it, is what he is sharing with us, SUCCESS, HAPPINESS, and mostly FREEDOM to all Health Professionals.

SYMPHONY OF SKILLS -001
BY Dr. BAK NGUYEN

You will enlighten the world with your potential. I can't wait to see all the differences that you will have in our world. Remember that power comes with responsibility. We can feel in his presence, a genuine force, a depth of energy, confidence, innocence, courage, and intelligence. Bak is always looking for answers, morning and night, he wants to understand the why and the why not. This book is the essence of the man. Dr. Bak is a force of nature who bears proudly his title eHappy. The man never ceases smiling nor spreading his good vibe wherever he passes. He is not trapped in the nostalgia of the past nor the satisfaction of the present, he embodies the joy of what's possible, what's to come. The more we read, the more we share, and we live. That is Bak, he charms us to evolve and to share his points of view, and before we know it, we are walking by his side, a journey we never saw coming.

T

THE 90 DAYS CHALLENGE -061
BY Dr. BAK NGUYEN

THE 90 DAYS CHALLENGE, is Dr. Bak's journey into the unknown. Overachiever writing 2 books a month on average, for the last 30 months, ambitious CEO, Industries' Disruptor, Dr. Bak seems to have success in everything he touches. Everything except the control of his weight. For nearly 20 years, he struggles with an overweight problem. Every time he scored big, he added on a little more weight. Well, this time, he exposes himself out there, in real-time and without filter, accepting the challenge of his brother-in-law, DON VO to lose 45 pounds within 90 days. That's half a pound a day, for three months. He will have to do so while keeping all of his other challenges on track, writing books at a world record pace, leading the dental industry into the new ERA, and keep seeing his patients. Undoubtedly entertaining, this is the journey of an ALPHA who simply won't give up. But this time, nothing is sure.

THE BOOK OF LEGENDS -024
BY Dr. BAK NGUYEN & WILLIAM BAK

The Book of Legends vol. 1 the story behind the world record of Dr. Bak and his son, William Bak. All Dr. Bak had in mind was to keep his promise of writing a book with his son. They ended up writing 8 children's books within a month, scoring a new world record. William is also the youngest author having published in two languages. Those are world records waiting to be confirmed. History will say: to celebrate a first world record (writing 15 books / 15 months), for the love of his son, he will have scored a second world record: to write 8 books within a month! THE BOOK OF LEGENDS vol. 1 This is both a magical journey for both a father and a son looking to connect and to find themselves. Join Dr. Bak and William Bak in their journey and their love for Life!

THE BOOK OF LEGENDS 2 -041
BY Dr. BAK NGUYEN & WILLIAM BAK

THE BOOK OF LEGENDS vol. 2 is the sequel of "CINDERELLA" but a true story between a father and his son. Together they have discovered a bond and a way to connect. The first BOOK OF LEGENDS covered the time of the first four books they wrote together within a month. The second BOOK OF LEGENDS is covering what happened after the curtains dropped, what happened after reality kicked back in. If the first volume was about a fairy tale in vacation time, the second volume is about making it last in real Life. Share their journey and their love of Life!

THE BOOK OF LEGENDS 3 -086
THE END OF THE INNOCENCE AGE
BY Dr. BAK NGUYEN & WILLIAM BAK

This is the third volume of the series, THE BOOK OF LEGENDS. If the first two happened as a breeze breaking world records on top of world records (27 books written as father and son), the 3rd volume took much more time to arrive. William has grown and writing chicken books is not enough anymore to ignite his imagination. Dr. Bak, as a good father, will try to follow William's growth and invented new games, technics and mind frames to keep engaging William's imagination and interest. From auditions to backstories, Dr. Bak bent backward to keep the adventure going. More than sharing the success and the glory, within THE BOOK OF LEGENDS volume 3, you are sharing the doubts and failure of a father and son refusing to let go... but who have now left MOMENTUM... until the winds blow once more in their favour. Welcome to the Alphas.

THE CONFESSION OF A LAZY OVERACHIEVER -089
REINVENT YOURSELF FROM ANY CRISIS
BY Dr. BAK NGUYEN

In THE CONFESSION OF A LAZY OVERACHIEVER, Dr. Bak is opening up to his new marketing officer, Jamie, fresh out of school. She is young, full of energy, and looking to chill and still to have it all. True to his character, Dr. Bak is giving Jamie some leeway to redefine Dr. Bak's brand to her demographic, the Millennials. This journey is about Dr. Bak satisfying the Millennials and answering their true questions in life. A rebel himself, his ambition to change the world started back on campus, some 25 years ago... then, life caught up with him. It took Dr. Bak 20 years to shake down the burdens of life, to spread his wings free from Conformity, and to start Overachieving. Doctor, CEO, and world record author, here is what Dr. Bak would have love to know 25 years ago as was still on campus. In a word, this is cheating your way to success and freedom. And yes, it is possible. Success, Money, Freedom, it all starts with a mindset and the awareness of Time. Welcome to the Alphas.

THE ENERGY FORMULA -053
BY Dr. BAK NGUYEN

THE ENERGY FORMULA is a book dedicated to help each individual to find the means to reach their purpose and goal in Life. Dr. Bak is a philosopher, a strategist, a business, an artist, and a dentist, how does he do all of that? He is doing so while mentoring proteges and leading the modernization of an entire industry. Until now, Momentum and Speed were the powers that he was building on and from. But those powers come from somewhere too. From a guide of our Quest of Identity, he became an ally in everyone's journey for happiness. THE ENERGY FORMULA is the book revealing step by step, the logic of building the right mindset and the way to ABUNDANCE and HAPPINESS, universally. It is not just a HOW TO book, but one that will change your life and guide you to the path of ABUNDANCE.

THE MODERN WOMAN -070
TO HAVE IT HAVE WITH NO SACRIFICE
BY Dr. BAK NGUYEN & Dr. EMILY LETRAN

In THE MODERN WOMAN: TO HAVE IT ALL WITH NO SACRIFICE, Dr. Bak joins forces with Dr. Emily Letran to empower all women to fulfill their desires, goals, and ambition. Both overachievers going against the odds, they are sharing their experience and wisdom to help all women to find confidence and support to redefine their lives. Dr. Emily Letran is a doctor in dentistry, an entrepreneur, author, and CERTIFIED HIGH-PERFORMANCE coach. For an Asian woman, she made it through the norms and the red tapes to find her voice. As she learned and grew with mentors, today she is sharing her secret with the energy that will motivate all of the female genders to stand for what they deserve. Alpha doctor, Bak is joining his voice and perspective since this is not about gender equality, but about personal empowerment and the quest of Identity of each, man and woman. Once more, Dr. Bak is bringing LEVERAGE and REASON to the new social deal between man and woman. This is not about gender, but about confidence.

THE POWER BEHIND THE ALPHA -008
BY TRANIE VO & Dr. BAK NGUYEN

It's been said by a "great man" that "We are born alone and we die alone." Both men and women proudly repeat those words as wisdom since. I apologize in advance, but what a fat LIE! That's what I learned and discovered in life since my mind and heart got liberated from the burden of scars and the ladders of society. I can have it all, not all at the same time, but I can have everything I put my mind and heart into. Actually, it is not completely true. I can have most of what I and Tranie put our minds into. Together, when we feel like one, there isn't much out of our reach. If I'm the mind, she's the heart; if I'm the Will, she's the means. Synergy is the core of our power.Tranie's aim is always Happiness. In Tranie's definition of life, there are no justifications, no excuses, no tomorrow. For Tranie, Happiness is measured by the minutes of every single day. This is why she's so strong and can heal people around her. That may also be why she doesn't need to talk much, since talking about the past or the future is, in her mind, dimming down the magic of the present, the Now. We both respect and appreciate that we are the whole balancing each other's equation of life, of love, of success. I was the plus and the minus, then I became the multiplication factor and grew into the exponential. And how is Tranie evolving in all of this? She is and always will be the balance. If anything, she is the equal sign of each equation.

THE POWER OF Dr. -066
THE MODERN TITLE OF NOBILITY
BY Dr. BAK NGUYEN, Dr. PAVEL KRASTEV AND COLLABORATORS

In THE POWER OF Dr., independent thinkers mean to exchange ideas. An idea can be very powerful if supported with a great work ethic. Work ethic, isn't that the main fabric of our white coats, scrubs, and title? In an era post-COVID where everything has been rebooted and that the healthcare industry is facing its own fate: to evolve or to be replaced, Dr. Bak and Dr. Pavel reveal the source of their power and their playbook to move forward, ahead.The power we all hold is our resilience and discipline. We put that for years at the service of our profession, from a surgical perspective. Now, we can harness that same power to rewrite the rules, the industry, and our future. Post-COVID, the rules are being rewritten, will you be part of the team or left behind?
"You can be in control!" More than personal growth and a motivational book, THE POWER OF Dr. is an awakening call to the doctor you look at when you graduate, with hope, with honour, with determination.

THE POWER OF YES -010
VOLUME ONE: IMPACT
BY Dr. BAK NGUYEN

In THE POWER OF YES, Dr. Bak is sharing his journey opening up and embracing the world, one day at a time, one ask at a time, one wish at a time. Far from a dare, saying YES allowed Dr. Bak to rewrite his mindsets and to break all the boundaries. This book is not one written a few days or weeks, but the accumulation of a journey for 12 months. The journeys started as Dr. Bak said YES to his producer to go on stage and to speak... That YES opened a world of possibilities. Dr. Bak embraced each and every one of them. 12 months later, he is celebrating the new world record of writing 9 books written over a period of 12 months. To him, it will be a miss, missing the 12 on 12 mark. To the rest of the world, they just saw the birth of a force of nature, the Alpha force. THE POWER OF YES is comprised of all the introduction of the adult books written by Dr. Bak within the first 12 months. Chapter by chapter, you can walk in his footstep seeing and smelling what he has. This is reality literature with a twist of POWER. THE POWER OF YES! Discover your potential and your power. This is the POWER OF YES, volume one. Welcome to the Alphas.

THE POWER OF YES 2 -037
VOLUME TWO: SHAPELESS
BY Dr. BAK NGUYEN

In THE POWER OF YES, volume 2, Dr. Bak is continuing his journey discovering his powers and influence. After 12 months embracing the world saying YES, he rose as an emerging force: he's been recognized as an INDUSTRIES DISRUPTOR, got nominated ERNST AND YOUNG ENTREPRENEUR OF THE YEAR, wrote 9 books within 12 months while launching the most ambitious private endeavour to reform his own industry, the dental field. Contender too many WORLD RECORDS, Dr. Bak is doing all of that in parallel. And yes, he is sleeping his nights and yes, he is writing his book himself, from the screen of his iPhone! Far from satisfied, Dr. Bak missed the mark of writing 12 books within 12 months and everything else is shaping and moving, and could come crumbling down at each turn. Now that Dr. Bak understands his powers, he is looking to test them and to push them to their limits, looking to keep scoring world records while materializing his vision and enterprises. This is the awakening of a Force of Nature looking to change the world for the better while having fun sharing. Welcome to the Alphas.

THE POWER OF YES 3 -046
VOLUME THREE: LIMITLESS
BY Dr. BAK NGUYEN

In THE POWER OF YES, volume 3, the journey of Dr. Bak continues where the last volume left, in front of 300 plus people showing up to his first solo event, a Dr. Bak's event. On stage and in this book, Dr. Bak reveals how 12 months saying YES to everything changed his life... actually, it was 18 months.
From a dentist looking to change the world from a dental chair into a multiple times world record author, the journey of openness is a rendez-vous with Fate. Dr. Bak is sharing almost in real-time his journey, experiences, but above all, his feelings, doubts, and comebacks. From one book to the next, from one journey to the next, follow the adventure of a man looking to find his name, his worth, and his place in the world. Doing so, he is touching people Doing so, he is touching people and initiating their rises. Are you ready for more? Are you ready to meet your Fate and Destiny? Welcome to the Alphas.

THE POWER OF YES 4 -087
VOLUME FOUR: PURPOSE
BY Dr. BAK NGUYEN

In THE POWER OF YES, volume 4, the journey continues days after where the last volume left. After setting the new world record of writing 48 books within 24 months, Dr. Bak is not ready to stop. As volume one covers 12 months of journey, volume 2 covers 6 months. Well, volume 3 covers 4 months. The speed is building up and increasing, steadily. This is volume 4, RISING, after breaking the sound barrier. Dr. Bak has reached a state where he is above most resistance and friction, he is now in a universe of his own, discovering his powers as he walks his journeys. This is no fiction story or wishful thinking, THE POWER OF YES is the journey of Dr. Bak, from one world record to the next, from one book to the next. You too can walk your own legend, you just need to listen to your innersole and to open up to the opportunity. May you get inspiration from the legendary journey of Dr. Bak and find your own Destiny. Welcome to the Alphas.

THE RISE OF THE UNICORN -038
BY Dr. BAK NGUYEN & Dr. JEAN DE SERRES

In THE RISE OF THE UNICORN, Dr. Bak is joining forces with his friend and mentor, Dr. Jean De Serres. Together both men had many achievements in their respective industries, but the advent of eHappyPedia, THE RISE OF THE UNICORN is a personal project dear to both of them: the QUEST OF HAPPINESS and its empowerment. This book is a special one since you are witnessing the conversation between two entrepreneurs looking to change the world by building unique tools and media. Just like any enterprise, the ride is never a smooth one in the park on a beautiful day. But this is about eHappyPedia, it is about happiness, right? So it will happen and with a smile attached to it! The unique value of this book is that you are sharing the ups and downs of the launch of a Unicorn, not just the glory of the fame, but also the doubts and challenges on the way. May it inspire you on your own journey to success and happiness.

THE RISE OF THE UNICORN 2 -076
eHappyPedia
BY Dr. BAK NGUYEN & Dr. JEAN DE SERRES

This is 2 years after starting the first tome. Dr. Bak's brand is picking up, between the accumulation of records and the recognition. eHappyPedia is now hot for a comeback. In THE RISE OF THE UNICORN 2, Dr. Bak is retracing and addressing each of Dr. Jean De Serres' concerns about the weakness of the first version of eHappyPedia and the eHappy movement. This is the sort of the creation and a UNICORN both in finance and in psychology. Never before, you will assist in such daily and decision-making process of a world phenomenon and of a company. Dr. Bak and Dr. De Serres are literally using the process of writing this series of books to plan and to brainstorm the birth of a bluechip. More than an intriguing story, this is the journey of 2 experienced entrepreneurs changing the world.

THE U.A.X STORY -072
THE ULTIMATE AUDIO EXPERIENCE
BY Dr. BAK NGUYEN

This is the story of the ULTIMATE AUDIO EXPERIENCE, U.A.X. Follow Dr. Bak's footstep on how he invented a new way to read and to learn. Dr. Bak brings his experience as a movie producer and a director to elevate the reading experience to another level with entertaining value and make it accessible to everyone, auditive, and visual people alike.

Three years plus of research and development, countless hours of trials and errors, Dr. Bak finally solved his puzzle: having written more than 1.1 million words. The irony is that he does not like to read, he likes audiobooks! U.A.X. finally allowed the opening of Dr. Bak's entire library to a new genre and media. U.A.X. is the new way to learn and enjoy Audiobooks. Made to be entertaining while keeping the self-educational value of a book, U.A.X. will appeal to both auditive and visual people. U.A.X. is the blockbuster of the Audiobooks. The format has already been approved by iTunes, Amazon, Spotify, and all major platforms for global distribution and streaming.

TIMING - TIME MANAGEMENT ON STEROIDS -074
BY Dr. BAK NGUYEN & WILLIAM BAK

In TIMING, TIME MANAGEMENT ON STEROIDS, Dr. Bak is sharing his secret to keep overachieving, overdelivering while raising the bar higher and higher. We all have 24 hours in a day, so how can some do so much more than others. Dr. Bak is not only sharing his secrets and mindset about time and efficiency, he is literally living his own words as this book is written within his last sprint to set the next world record of writing 100 books within 4 years, with only 31 days to go. With 8 books to write in 31 days, that's a little less than 4 days per book! Share the journey of a man surfing the change and looking to see where is the limit of the human mind, writing. In the meantime, understand his leverage, mindset, and secrets to challenge your own limits and dreams.

THE VACCINE -077
BY Dr. BAK NGUYEN & WILLIAM BAK

In THE VACCINE, A TALE OF SPIES AND ALIENS, Dr. Bak reprise his role as mentor to William, his 10 years-old son, both as co-author and as doctor. William is living through the COVID war and has accumulated many, many questions. That morning, they got out all at once. From a conversation between father and son, Dr. Bak is making science into words keeping the interest of his son a Saturday morning in bed. William is not just an audience, he is responsible to map the field with his questions. What started as a morning conversation between father and son, became within the next hour, a great project, their 23rd book together. Learn about the virus, vaccination while entertaining your kids.

TO OVERACHIEVE EVERYTHING BEING LAZY -090
CHEAT YOUR WAY TO SUCCESS
BY Dr. BAK NGUYEN

In TO OVERACHIEVE EVERYTHING BEING LAZY, Dr. Bak retaking his role talking to the millennials, the next generation. If in the first tome of the series LAZY, Dr. Bak addresses the general audience of millennials, especially young women, he is dedicating this tome to the ALPHA amongst the millennials, those aiming for the moon and looking, not only to be happy but to change the world. This is not another take on how to cheat your way to success or how to leverage laziness, but this is the recipe to build overachievers and rainmakers. For the young leaders with ambitions and talent, understanding TIME and ENERGY are crucial from your first steps writing your our legend. If Dr. Bak had the chance to do it all over again, this is how he would do it! Welcome to the Alphas.

TORNADO -067
FORCE OF CHANGE
BY Dr. BAK NGUYEN

In TORNADO - FORCE OF CHANGE Dr. Bak is writing solo. In the midst of the COVID war, change is not a good intention anymore. Change, constant change has become a new reality, a new norm. From somebody who holds the title of Industries' Disruptor, how does he yield change to stay in control? Well, the changes from the COVID war are constant fear and much loss of individual liberty. Some can endure the change, some will ride it. Dr. Bak is sharing his angle of navigating the changes, yielding the improvisations, and to reinvent the goals, the means to stay relevant. From fighting to keep his companies Dr. Bak went on to let go the uncontrollable to embrace the opportunity, he reinvented himself to ride the change and create opportunities from an unprecedented crisis. This is the story of a man refusing to kneel and accept defeat, smiling back at faith to find leverage and hope.

TOUCHSTONE -073
LEVERAGING TODAY'S PSYCHOLOGICAL SMOG
BY Dr. BAK NGUYEN & Dr. KEN SEROTA

TOUCHSTONE, LEVERAGING TODAY'S PSYCHOLOGICAL SMOG is mapping to navigate and to thrive in today's high and constant stress environment. After 40 years in practice, Dr. Serota is concerned about the evolution of the career of health care professionals and the never-ending level of stress. What is stress, what are its effects, damages, and symptoms? If COVID-19 revealed to the world that we are fragile, it also revealed most of the broken and the flaws of our system. For now a century, dentistry has been a champion in depression, Dr.ug addiction, and suicide rate, and the curve is far from flattening. Dr. Bak is sharing his perspective and experience dealing with stress and how to leverage it into a constructive force. From the stress of a doctor with no right to failure to the stress of an entrepreneur never knowing the future, Dr. Bak is sharing his way to use stress as leverage.

From Canada, **Dr BAK NGUYEN**, Nominee Ernst and Young Entrepreneur of the year, Grand Homage Lys DIVERSITY, and LinkedIn & TownHall Achiever of the year. Dr Bak is a cosmetic dentist, CEO and founder of Mdex & Co. His company is revolutionizing the dental field. Speaker and motivator, he wrote 72 books over 36 months accumulating many world records (to be officialized).

- **ENTREPRENEURSHIP**
- **LEADERSHIP**
- **QUEST OF IDENTITY**
- **DENTISTRY AND MEDICINE**
- **PARENTING**
- **CHILDREN BOOKS**
- **PHILOSOPHY**

In 2003, he founded Mdex, a dental company upon which in 2018, he launched the most ambitious private endeavour to reform the dental industry, Canada wide. Philosopher, he has close to his heart the quest of happiness of the people surrounding him, patients and colleagues alike. In 2020, he launched an International collaborative initiative named **THE ALPHAS** to share knowledge and for Entrepreneurs and Doctors to thrive through the Greatest Pandemic and Economic depression of our time.

In 2016, he co-found with Tranie Vo, Emotive World Incorporated, a tech research company to use technology to empower happiness and sharing. U.A.X. the ultimate audio experience is the landmark project on which the team is advancing, utilizing the technics of the movie industry and the advancement in ARTIFICIAL INTELLIGENCE to save the book industry and to upgrade the continuing education space.

These projects have allowed Dr Nguyen to attract interests from the international and diplomatic community and he is now the center of a global discussion in the wellbeing and the future of the health profession. It is in that matter that he shares his thoughts and encourages the health community to share their own stories.

"It's not worth it go through it alone! Together, we stand, alone, we fall."

Motivational speaker and serial entrepreneur, philosopher and author, from his own words, Dr Nguyen describes himself as a dentist by circumstances, an entrepreneur by nature and a communicator by passion.

He also holds recognitions from the Canadian Parliament and the Canadian Senate.

www.DrBakNguyen.com

UAX

ULTIMATE AUDIO EXPERIENCE

A new way to learn and enjoy Audiobooks. Made to be entertaining while keeping the self-educational value of a book, UAX will appeal to both auditive and visual people. UAX is the blockbuster of the Audiobooks.

UAX will cover most of Dr Bak's books, and is now negotiating to bring more authors and more titles to the UAX concept. Now streaming on Spotify, Apple Music and available for download on all major music platforms. Give it a try today!

AMAZON - BARNES & NOBLE - APPLE BOOKS - KINDLE
SPOTIFY - APPLE MUSIC

FROM THE SAME AUTHOR
Dr Bak Nguyen

www.DrBakNguyen.com

MAJOR LEAGUES' ACCESS

BUSINESS

CHILDREN'S BOOK
with William Bak

The Trilogy of Legends

THE SPIES AND ALIENS COLLECTION

MILLION DOLLAR MINDSET

PARENTING

PERSONAL GROWTH

PHILOSOPHY

SHORTCUT   SOCIETY

046 - THE POWER OF YES 3
VOLUME THREE: LIMITLESS
BY Dr BAK NGUYEN

087 - THE POWER OF YES 4
VOLUME FOUR: PURPOSE
BY Dr BAK NGUYEN

THE POWER OF YES - 010
VOLUME ONE: IMPACT
BY Dr BAK NGUYEN

091 - THE POWER OF YES 5
VOLUME FIVE: ALPHA
BY Dr BAK NGUYEN

THE POWER OF YES 2 - 037
VOLUME TWO: SHAPELESS
BY Dr BAK NGUYEN

092 - THE POWER OF YES 6
VOLUME SIX: PERSPECTIVE
BY Dr BAK NGUYEN

TITLES AVAILABLE AT
www.DrBakNguyen.com

AMAZON - BARNES & NOBLE - APPLE BOOKS - KINDLE
SPOTIFY - APPLE MUSIC

DR.

Bak Nguyen